# COLORING BOOK FOR GROWN UPS
## GEOMETRIC PATTERNS



Stress Relief & Relaxation

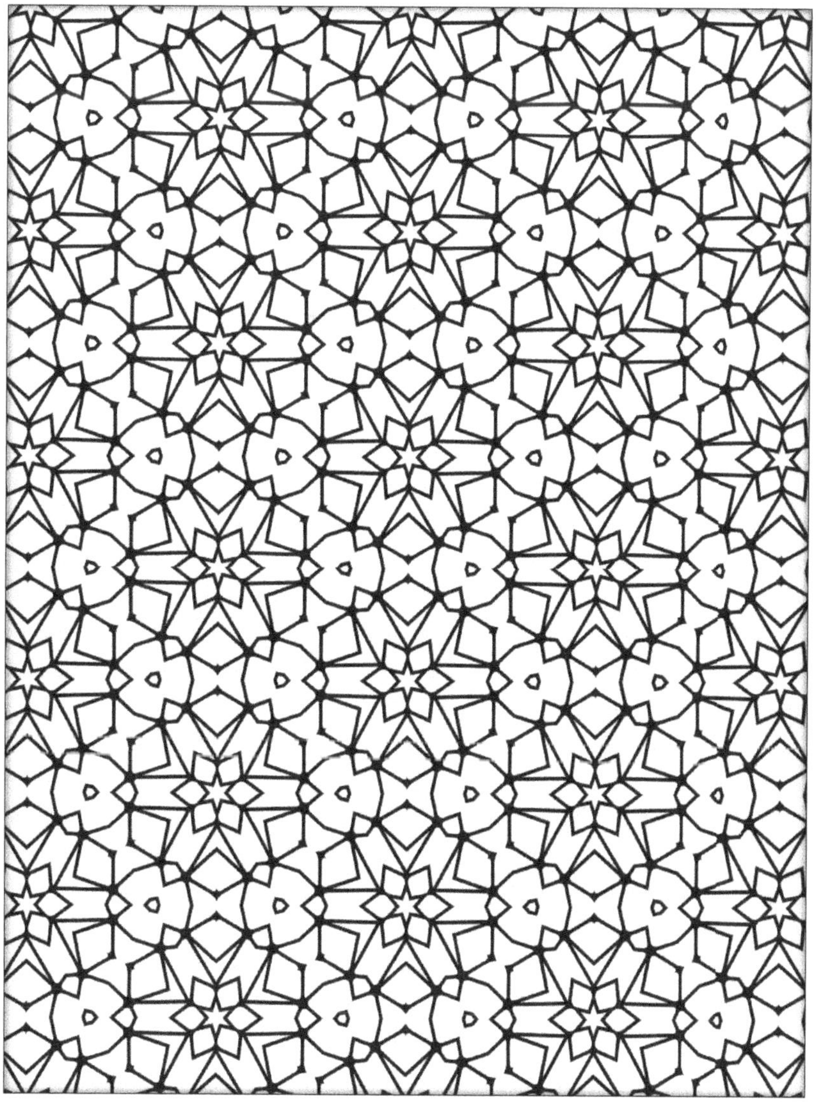

Over 40 Dazzling Abstract Patterns

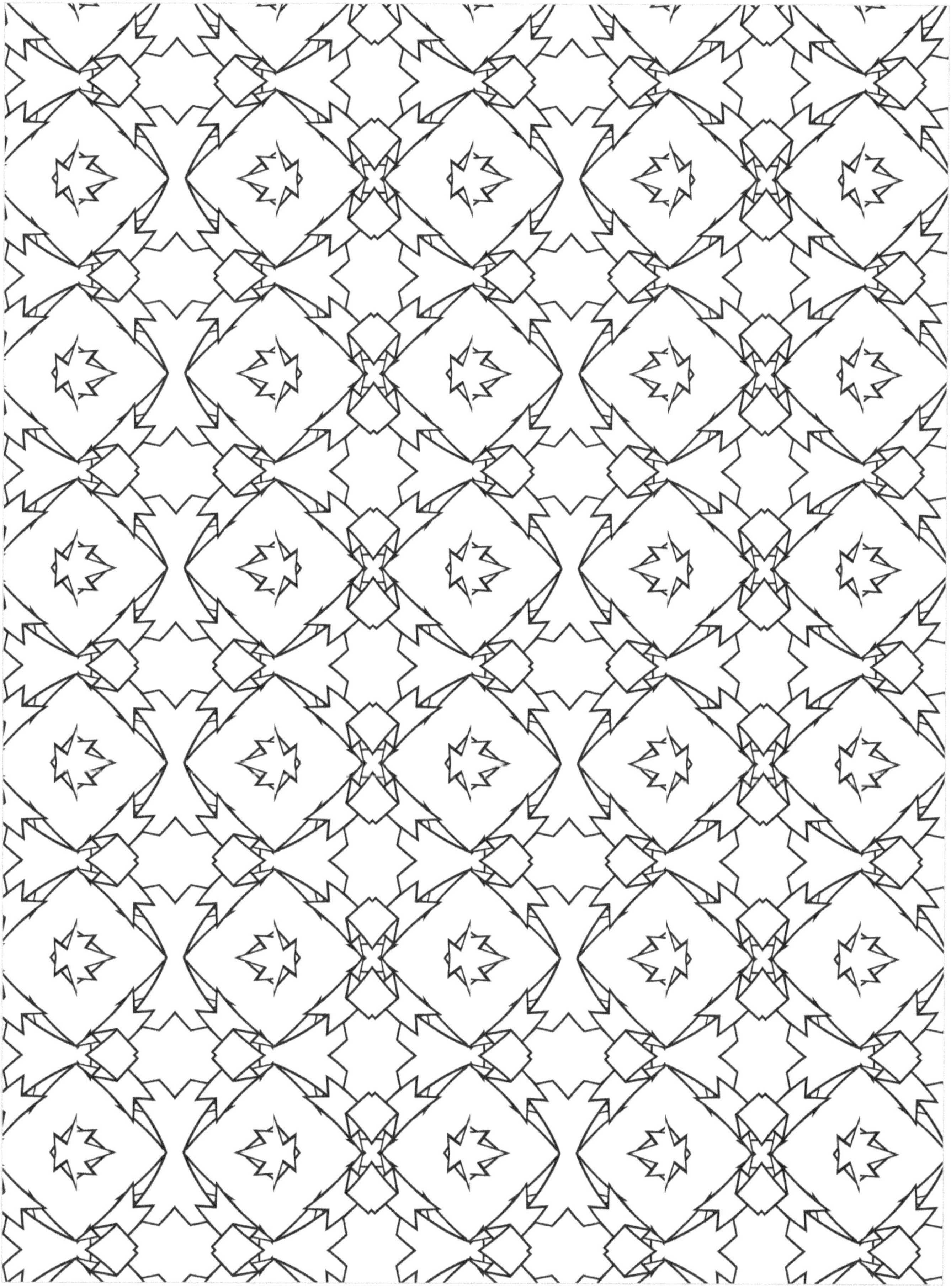

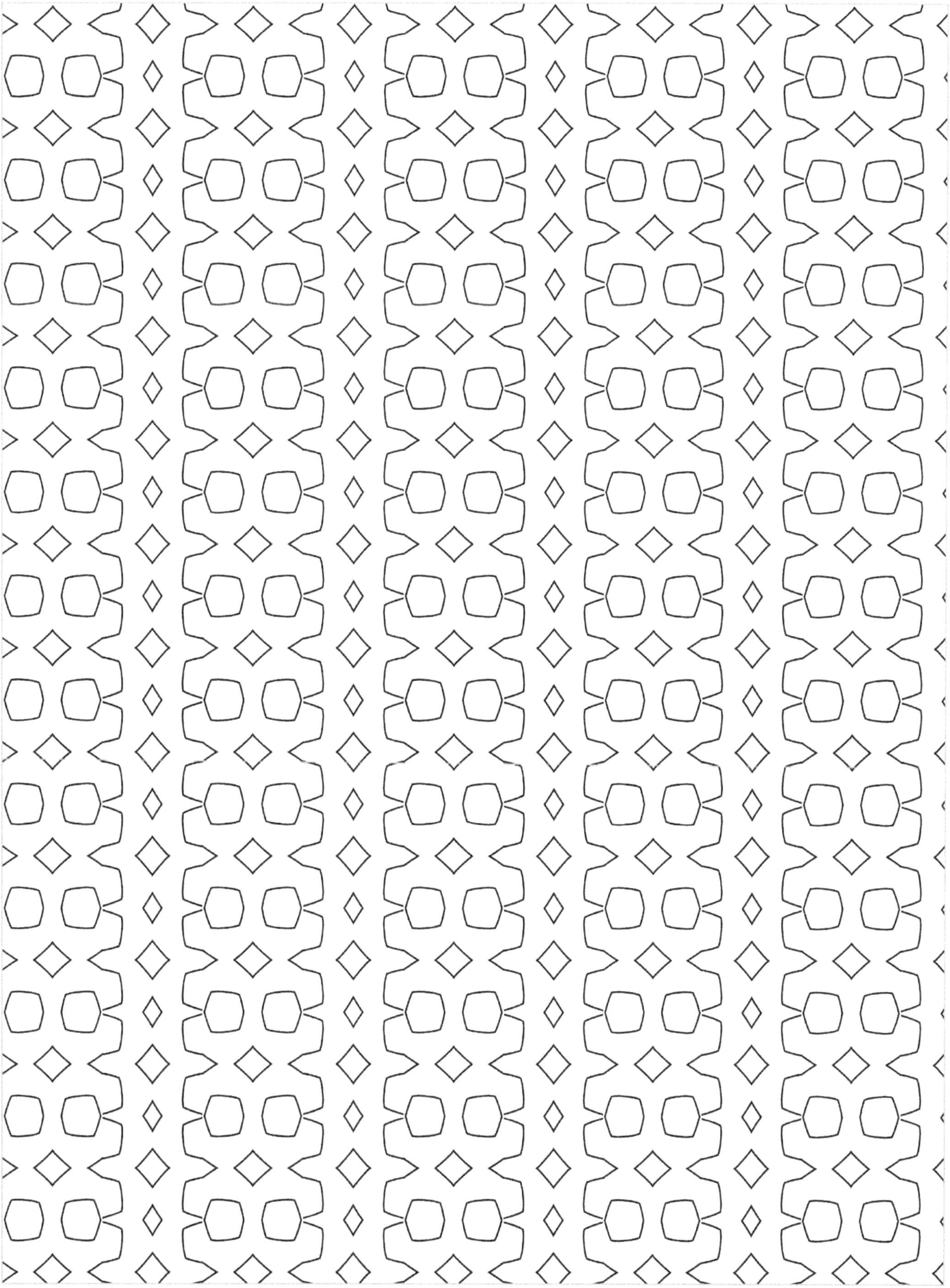

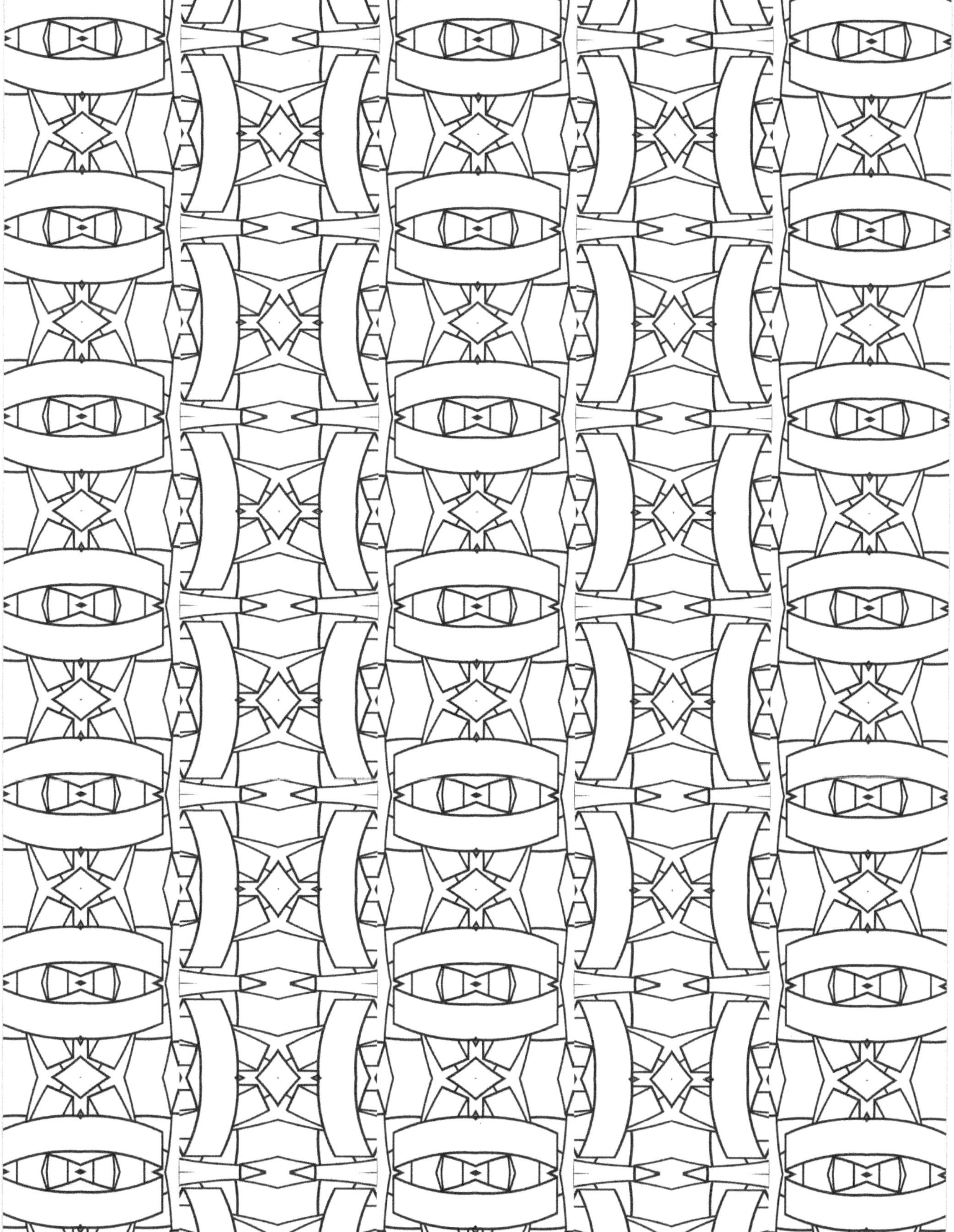

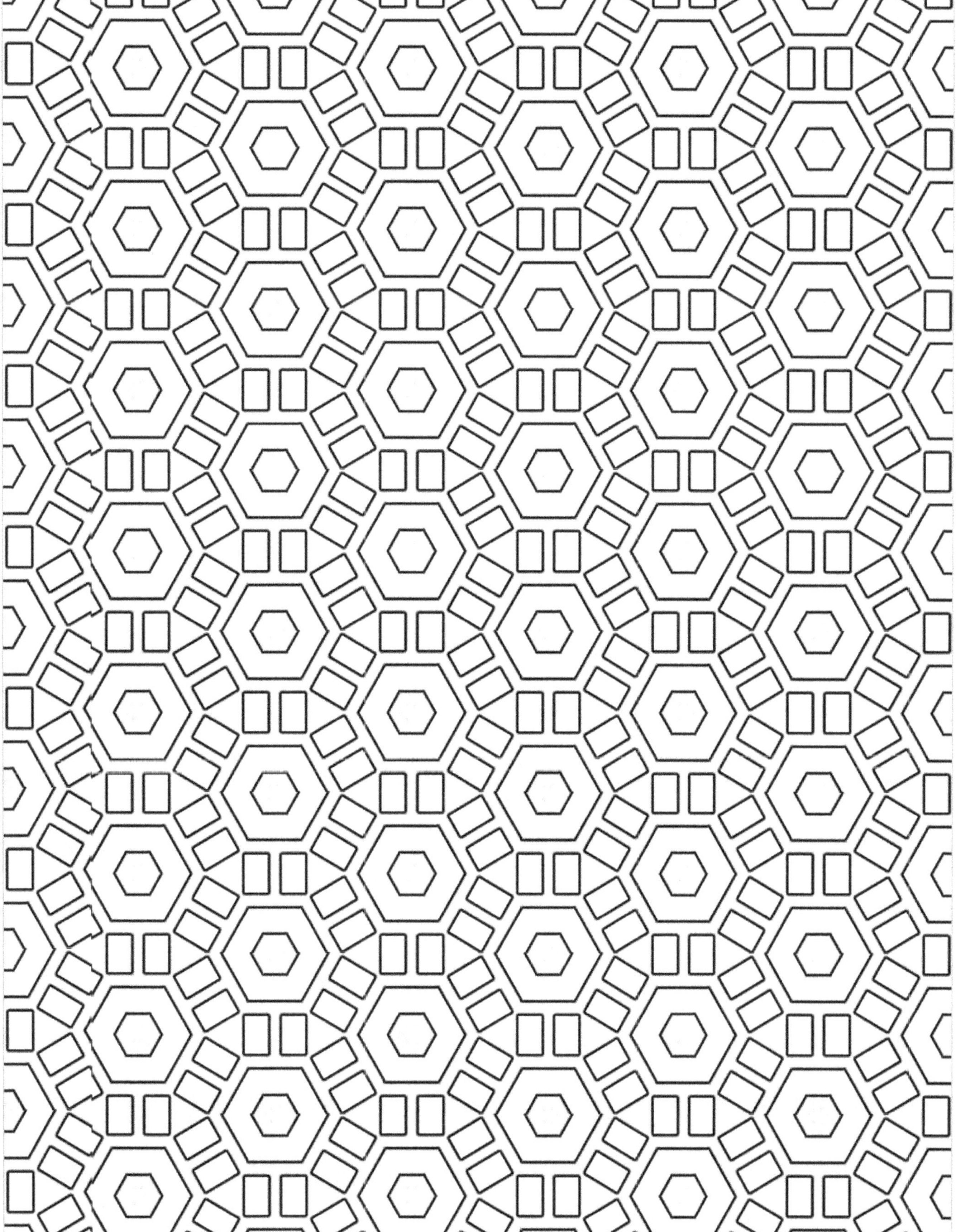

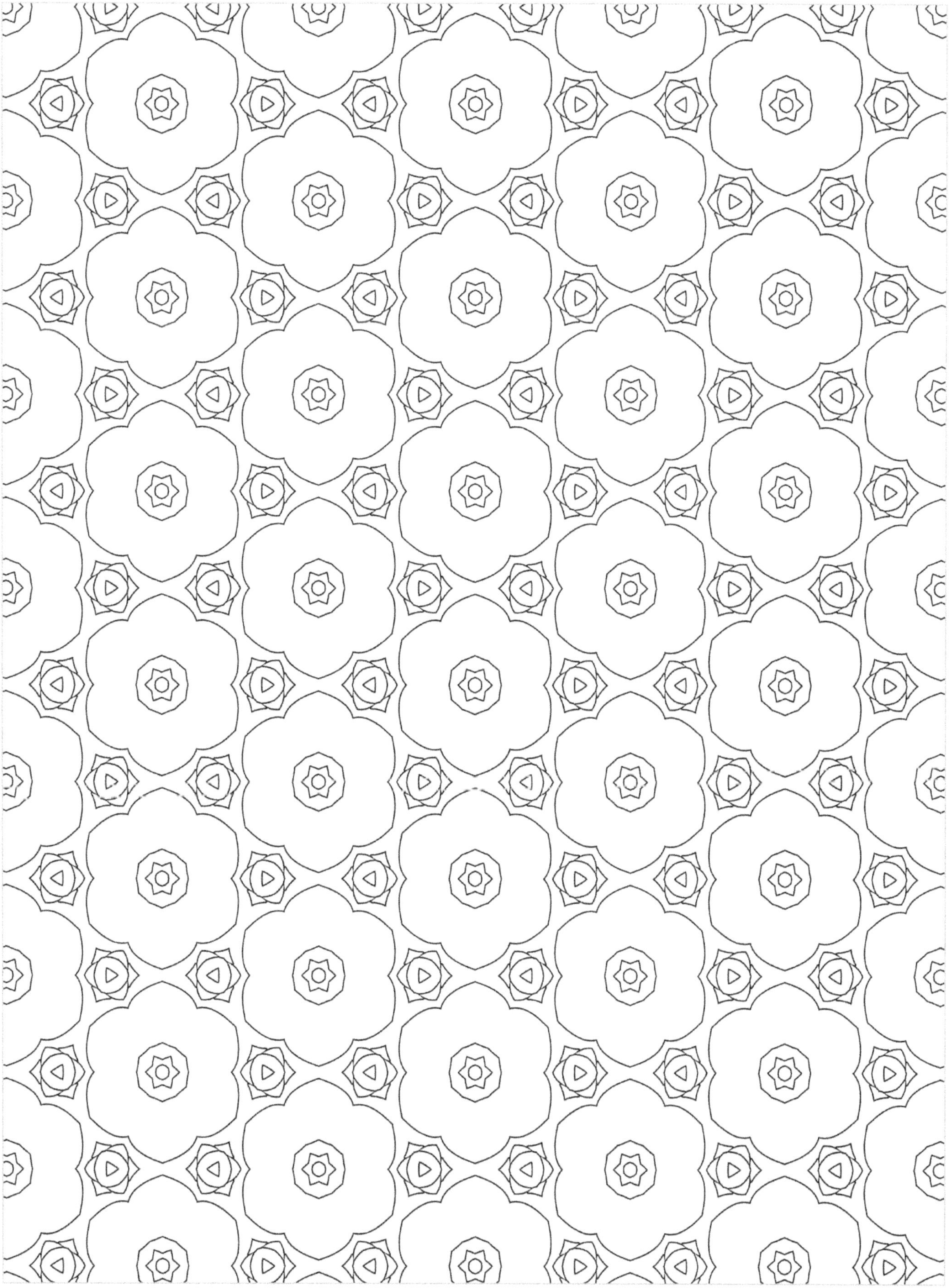

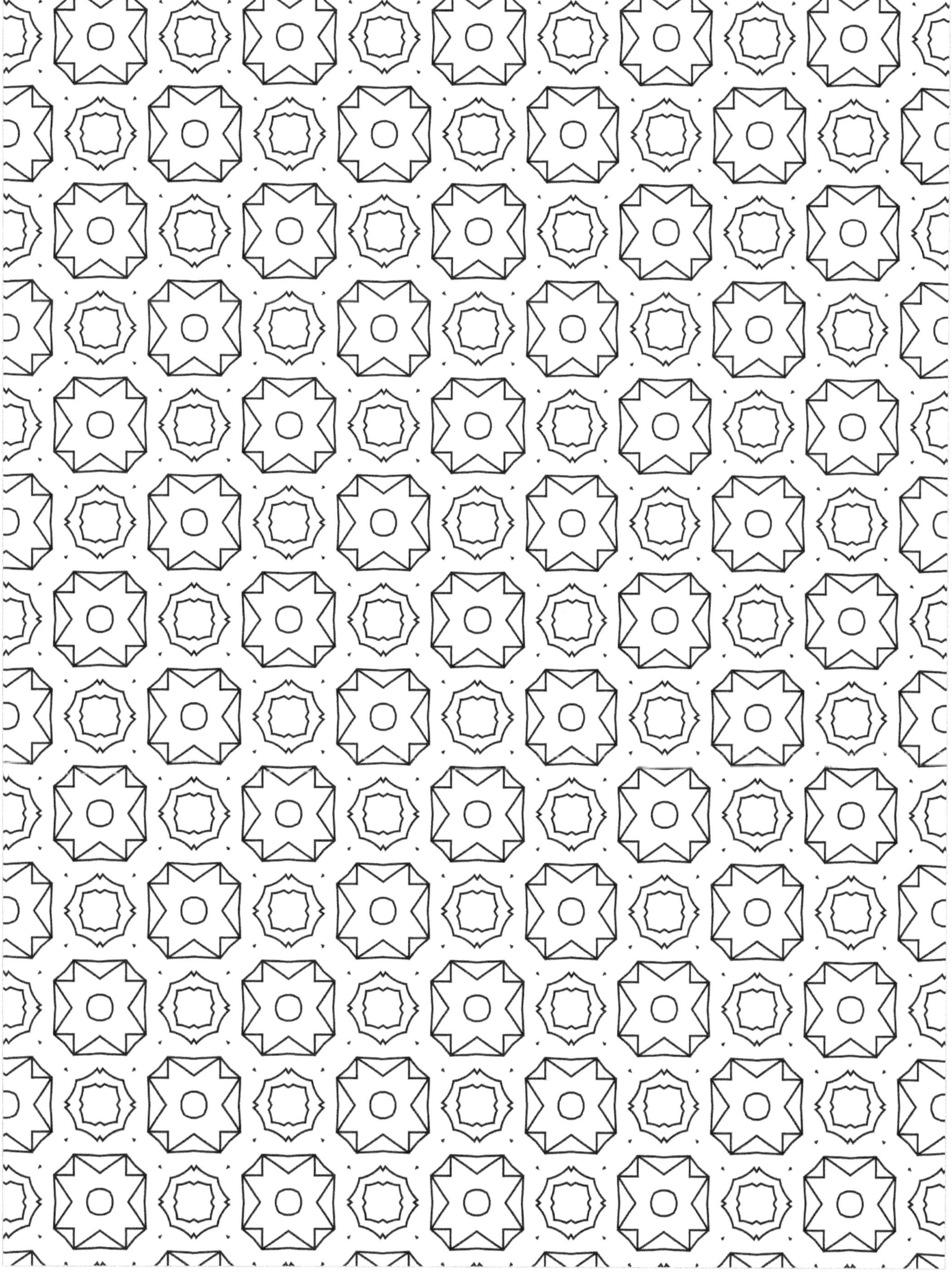

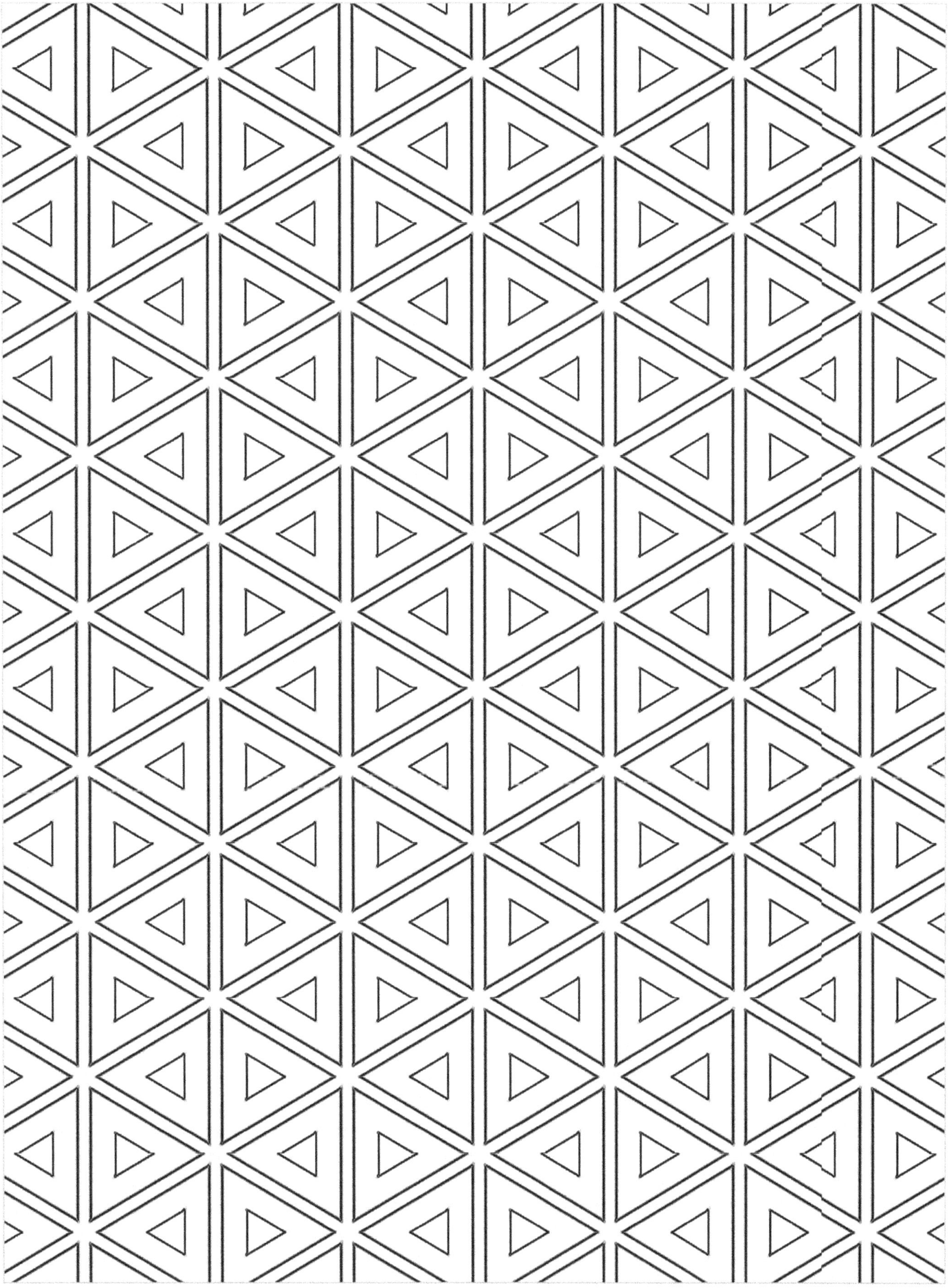

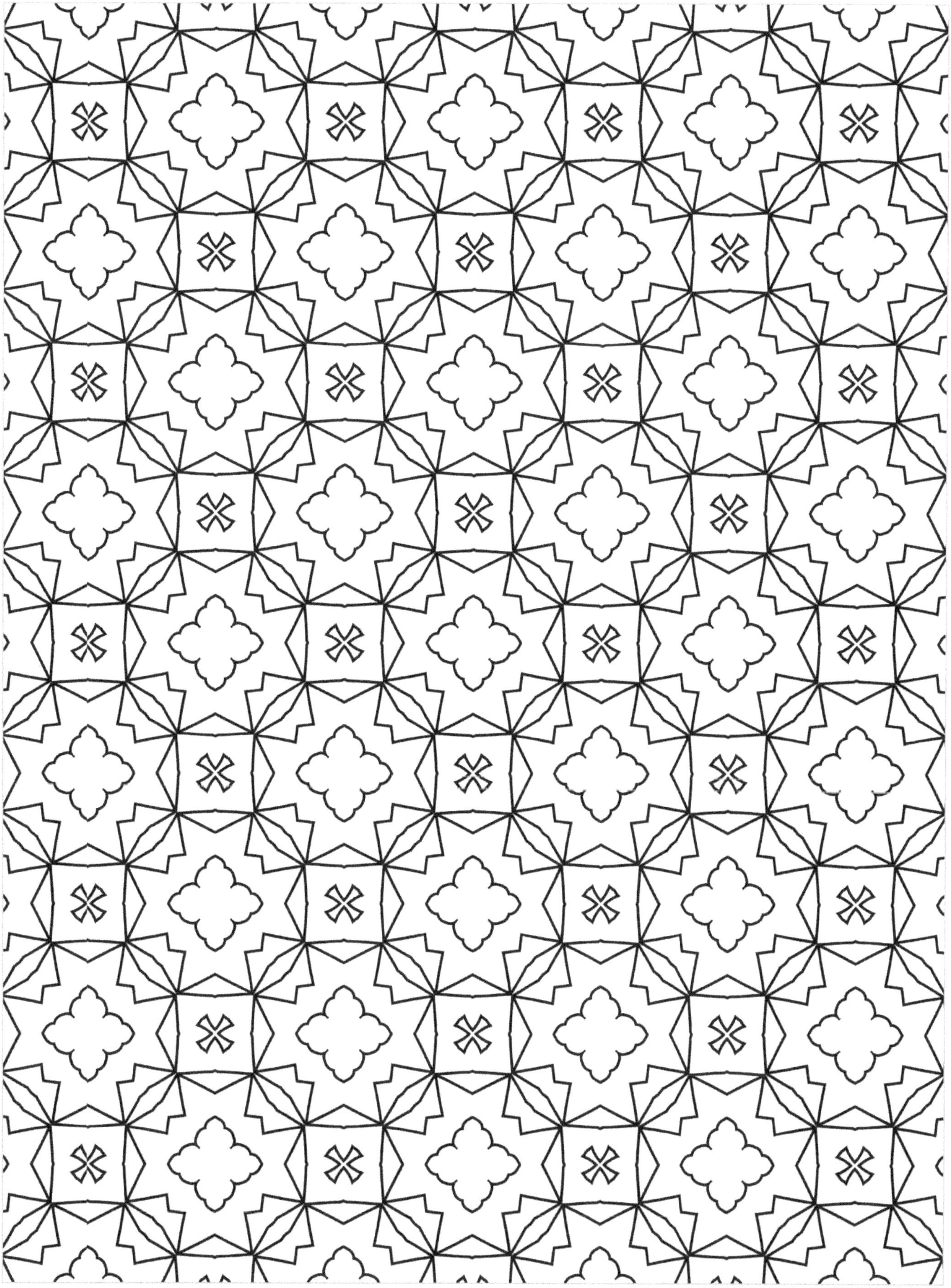

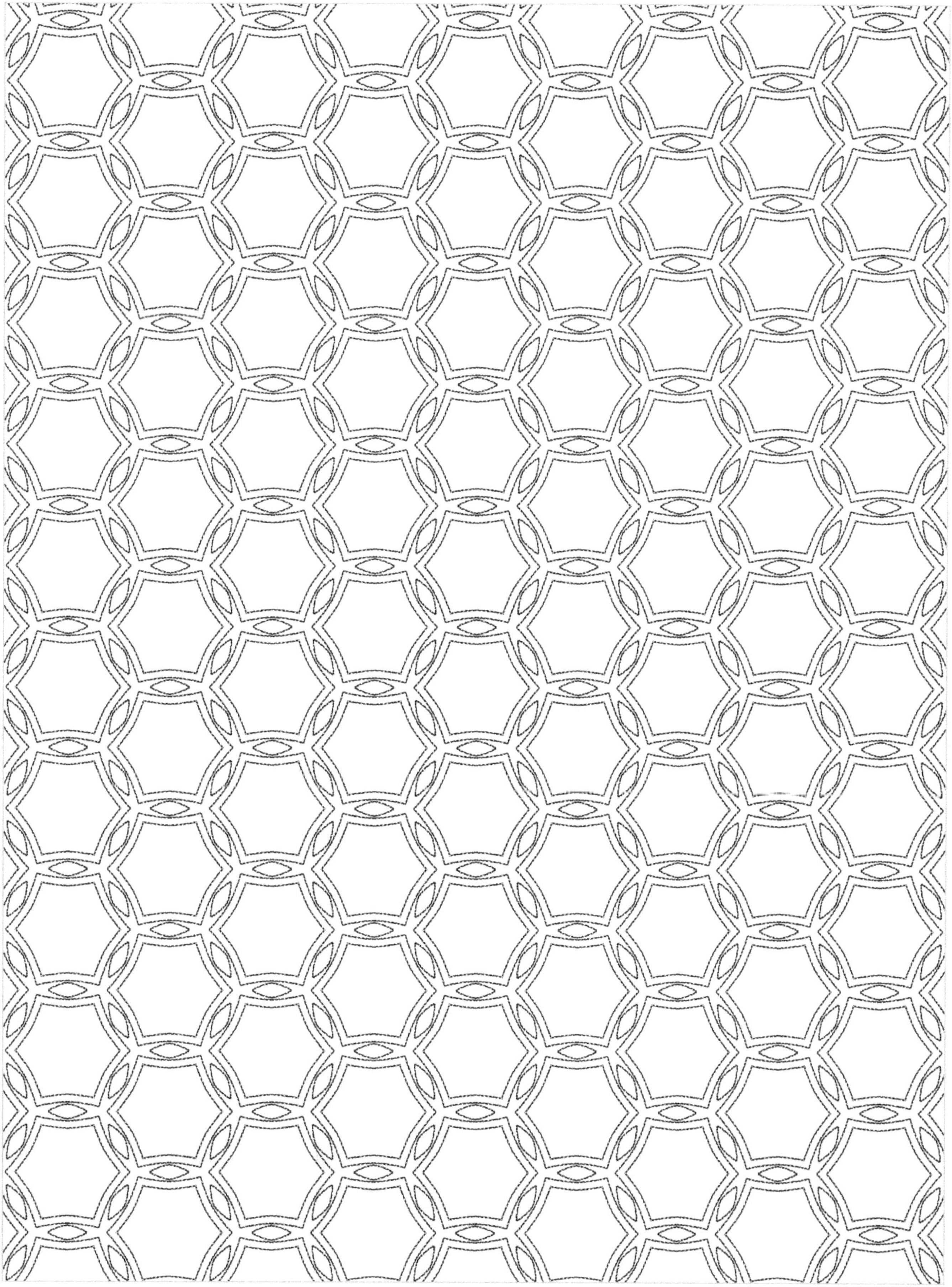

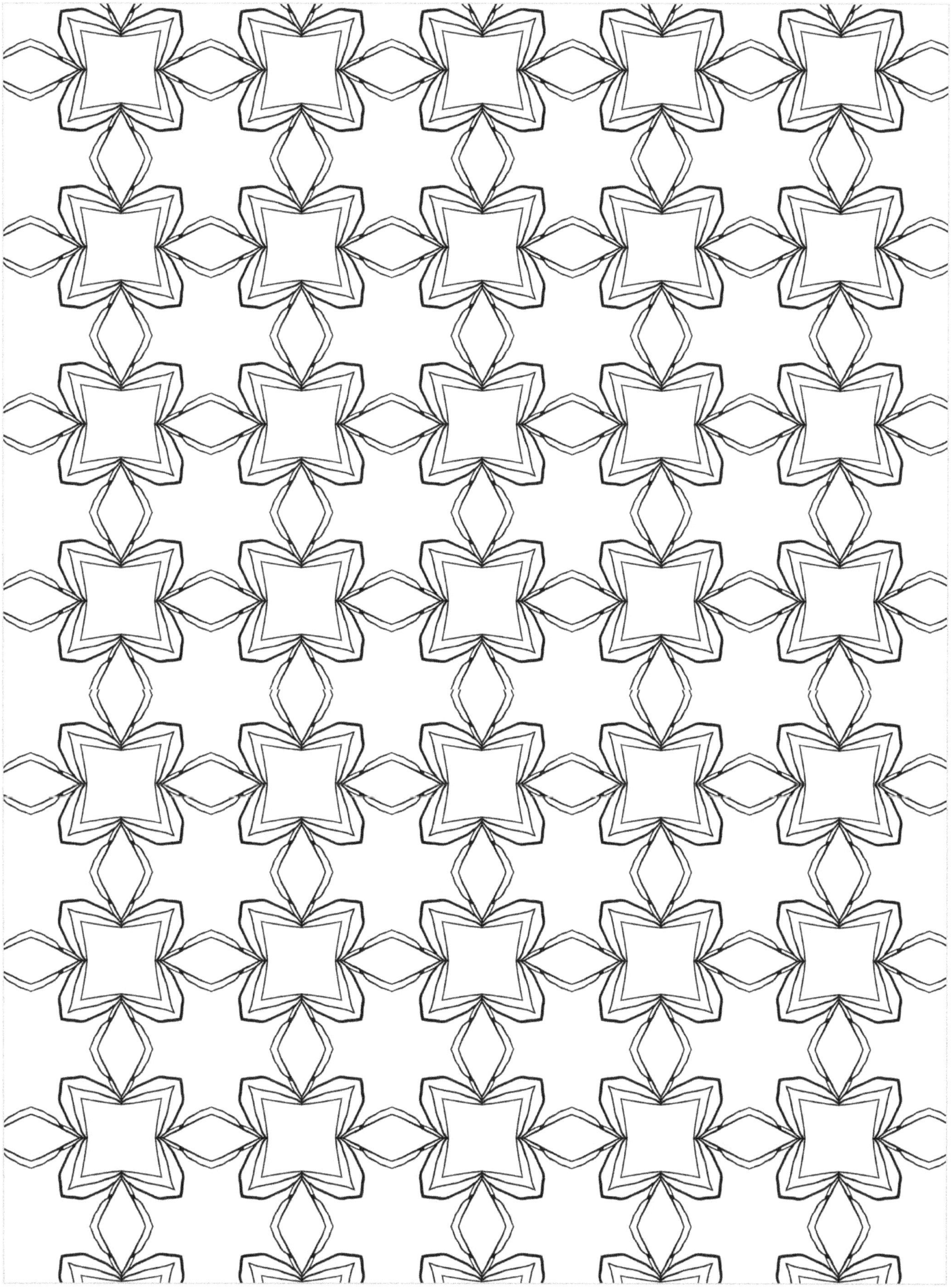

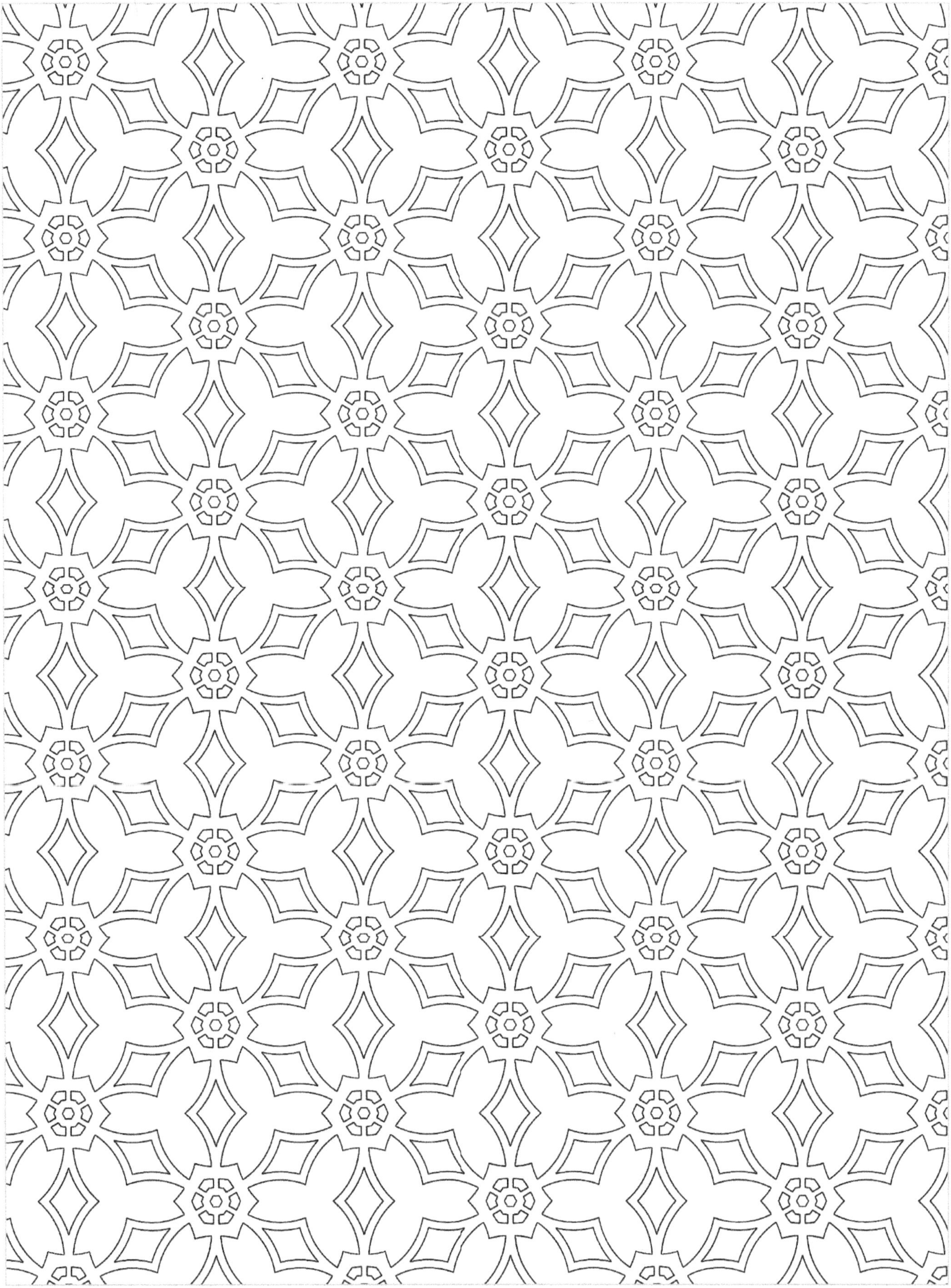

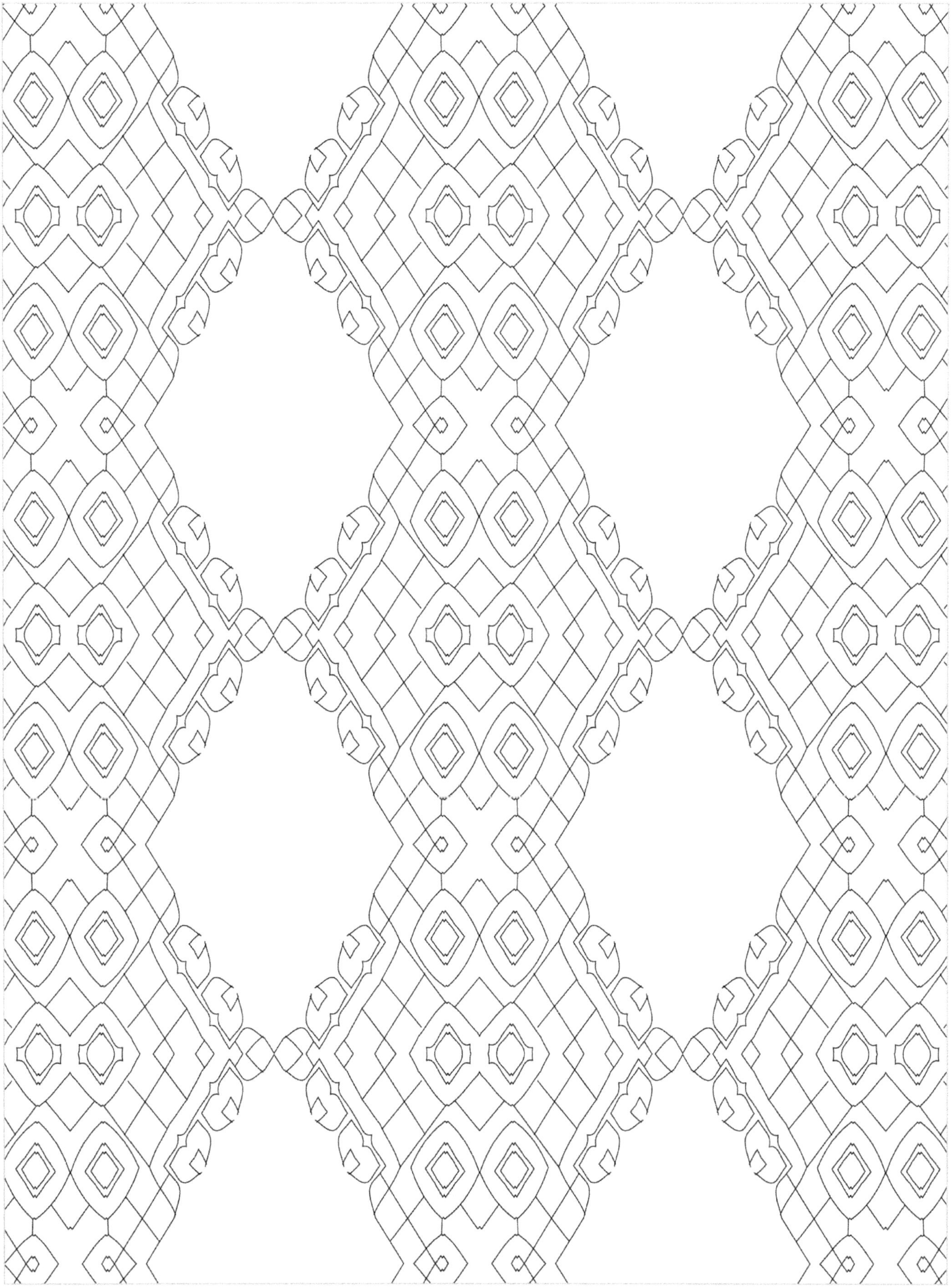

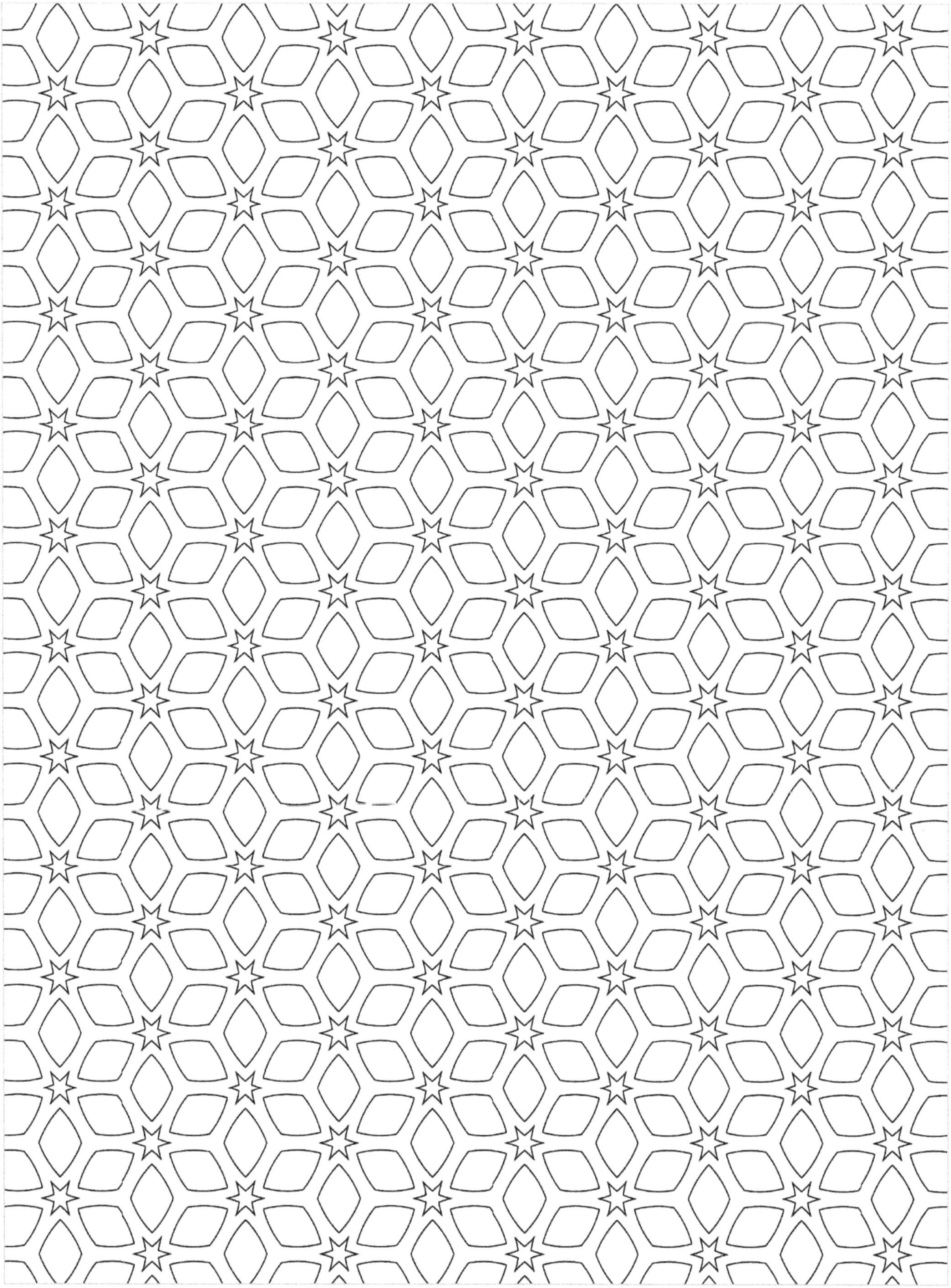

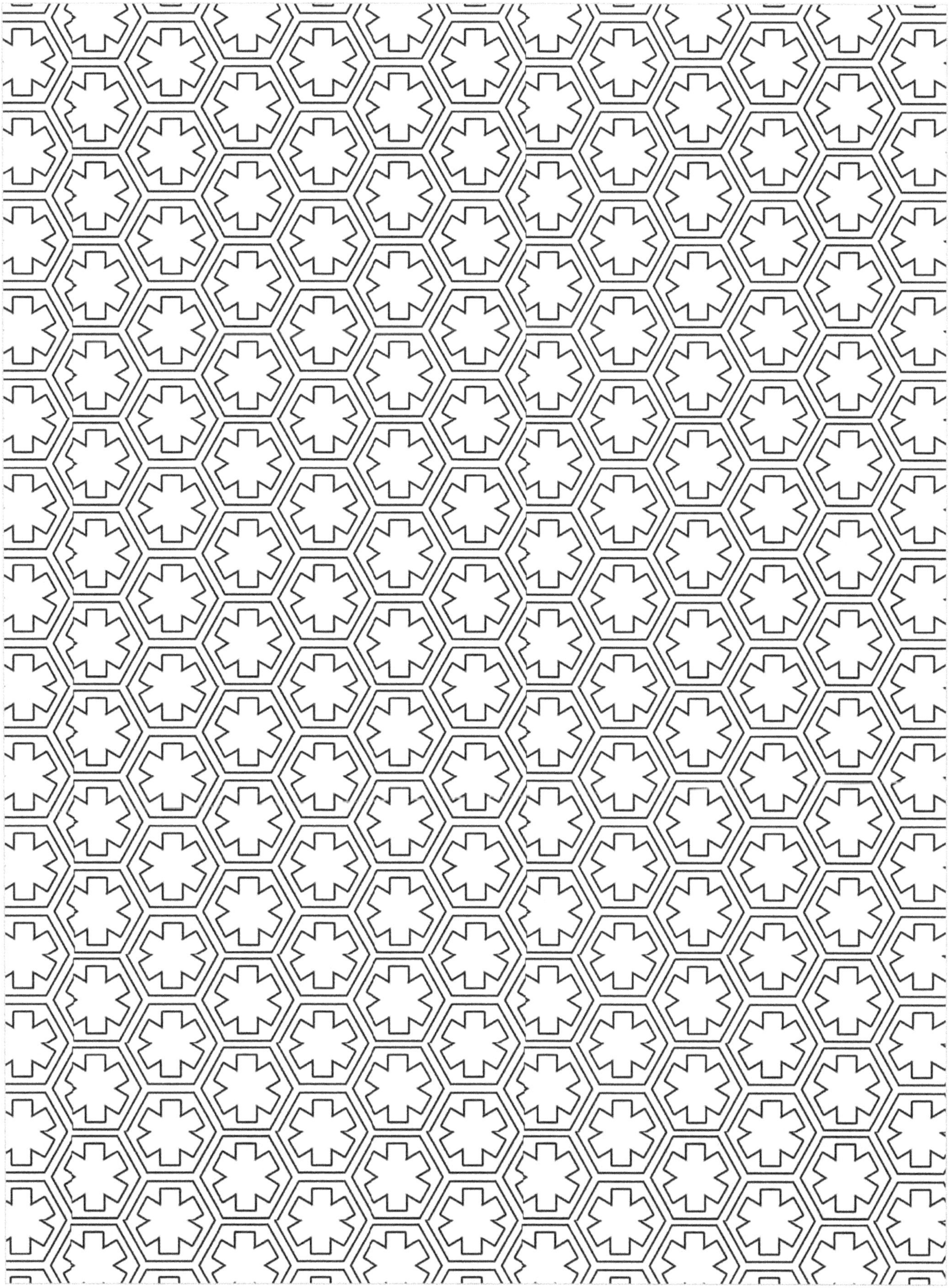

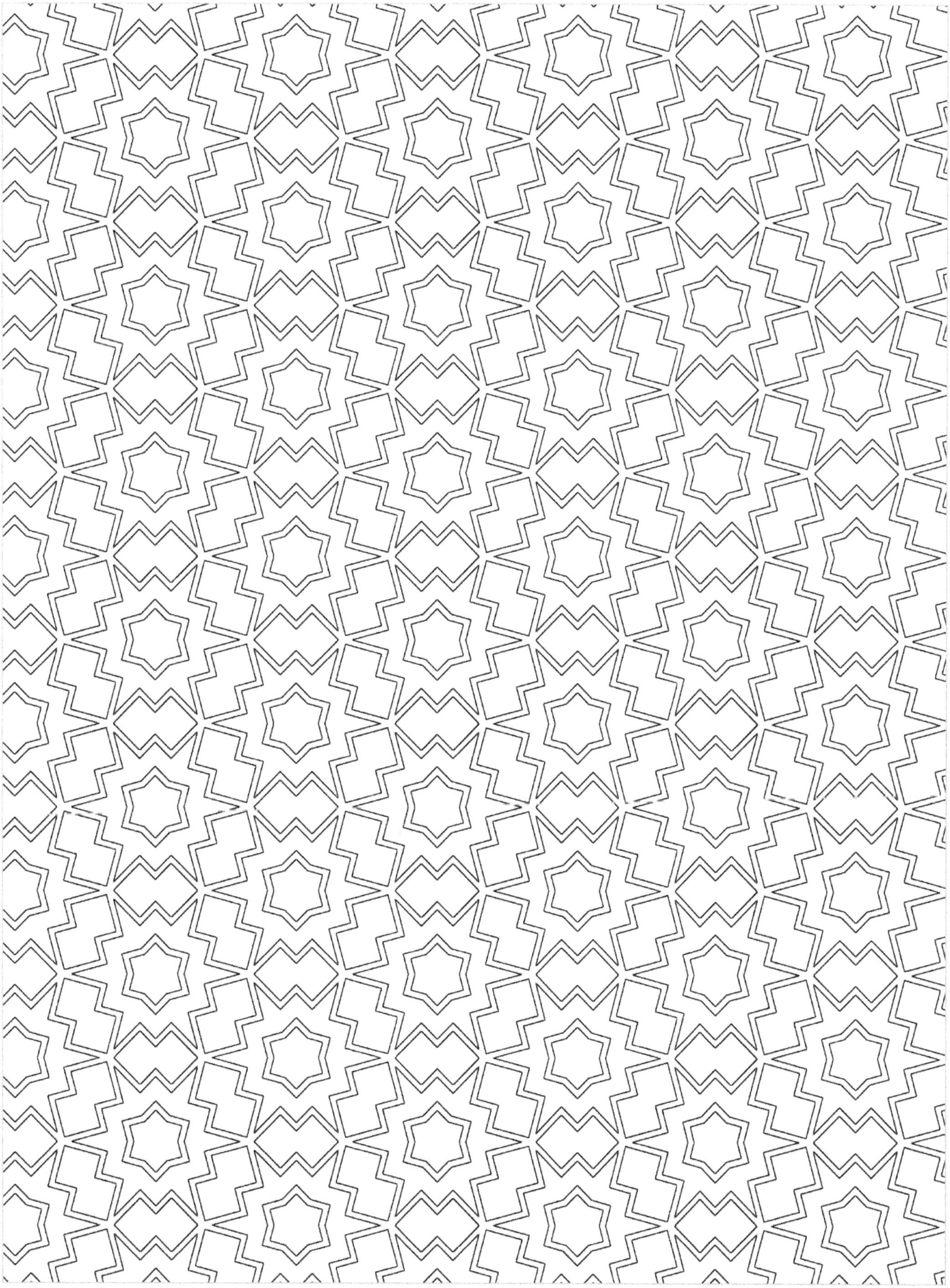

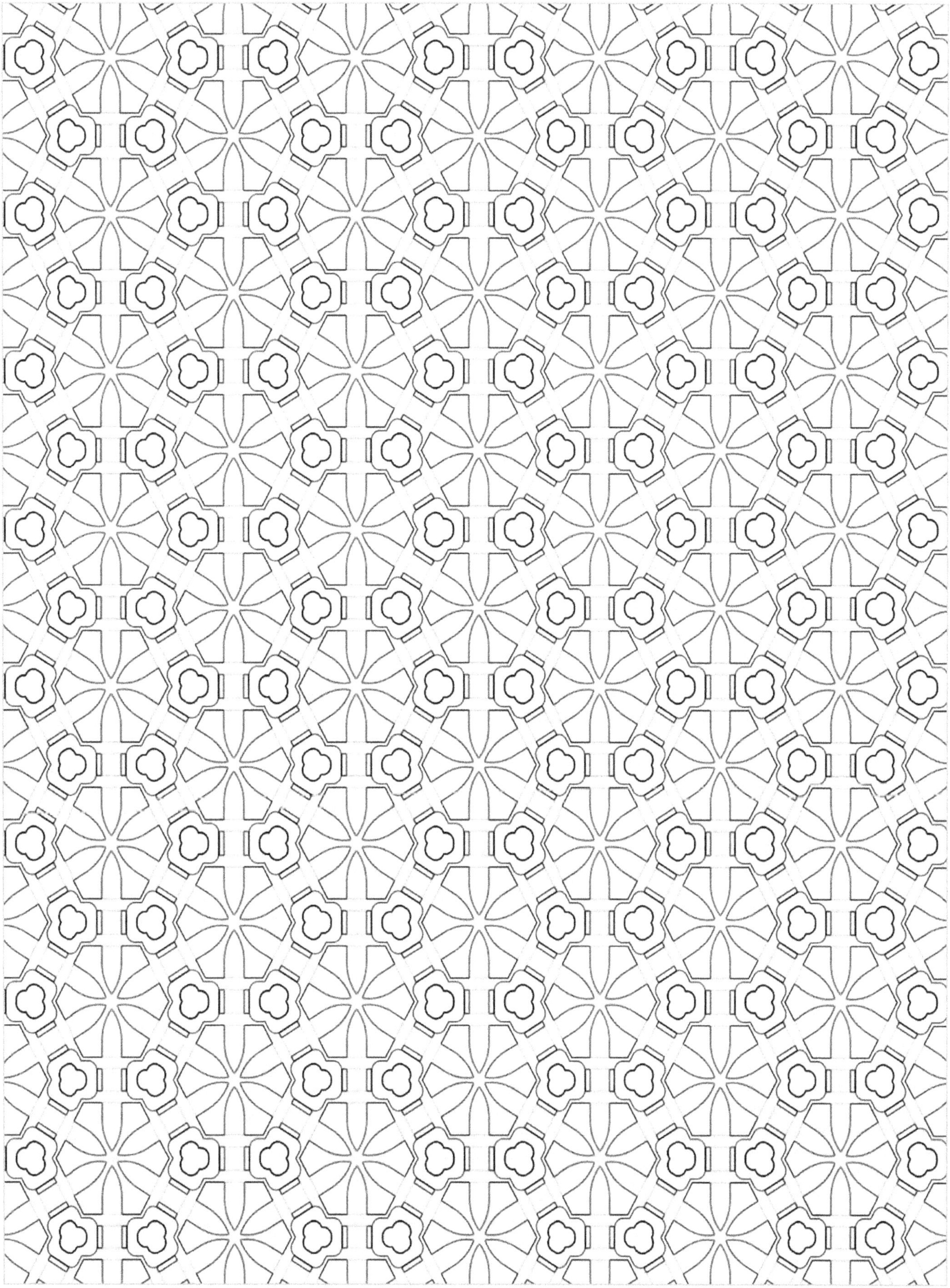

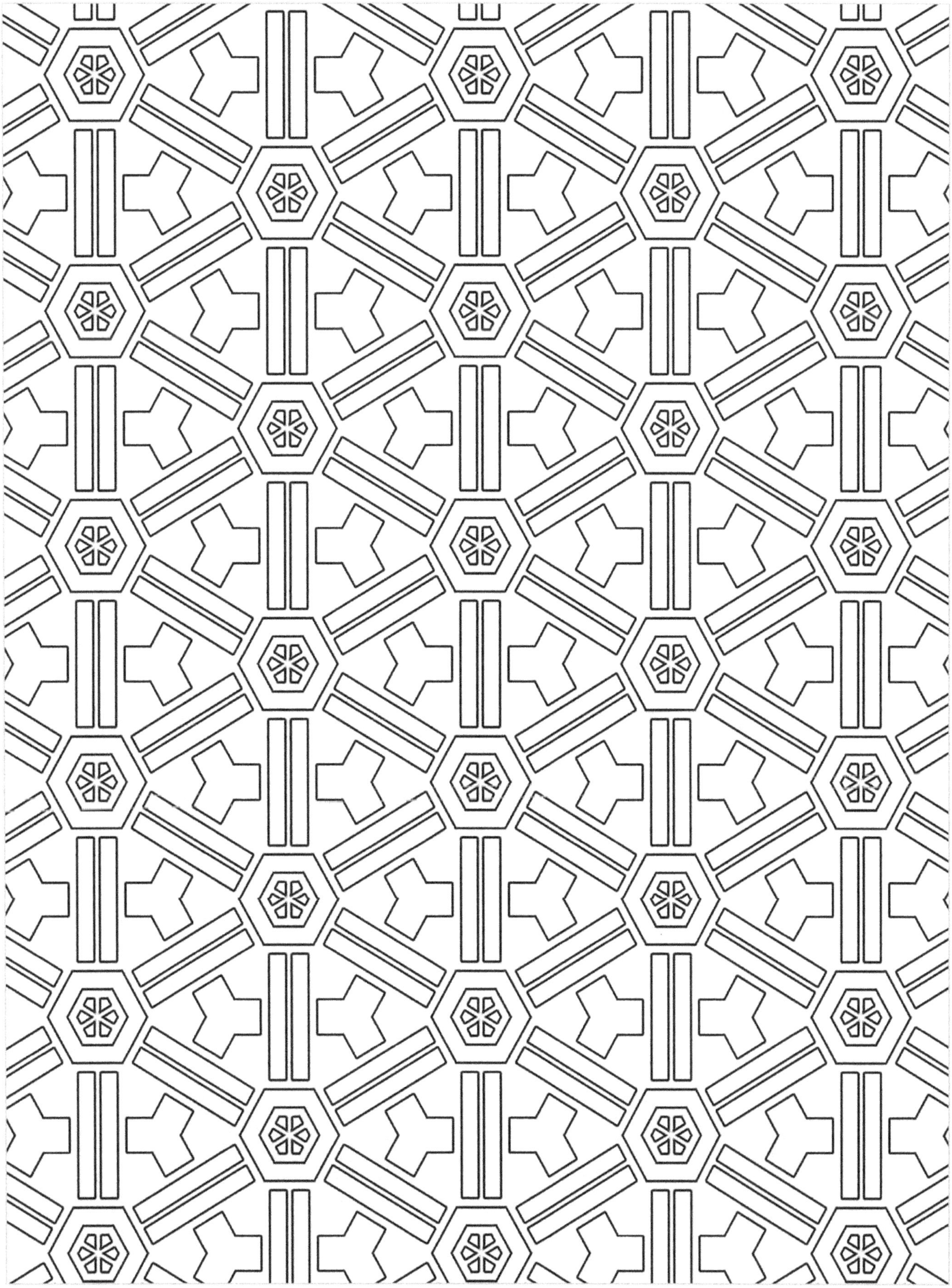

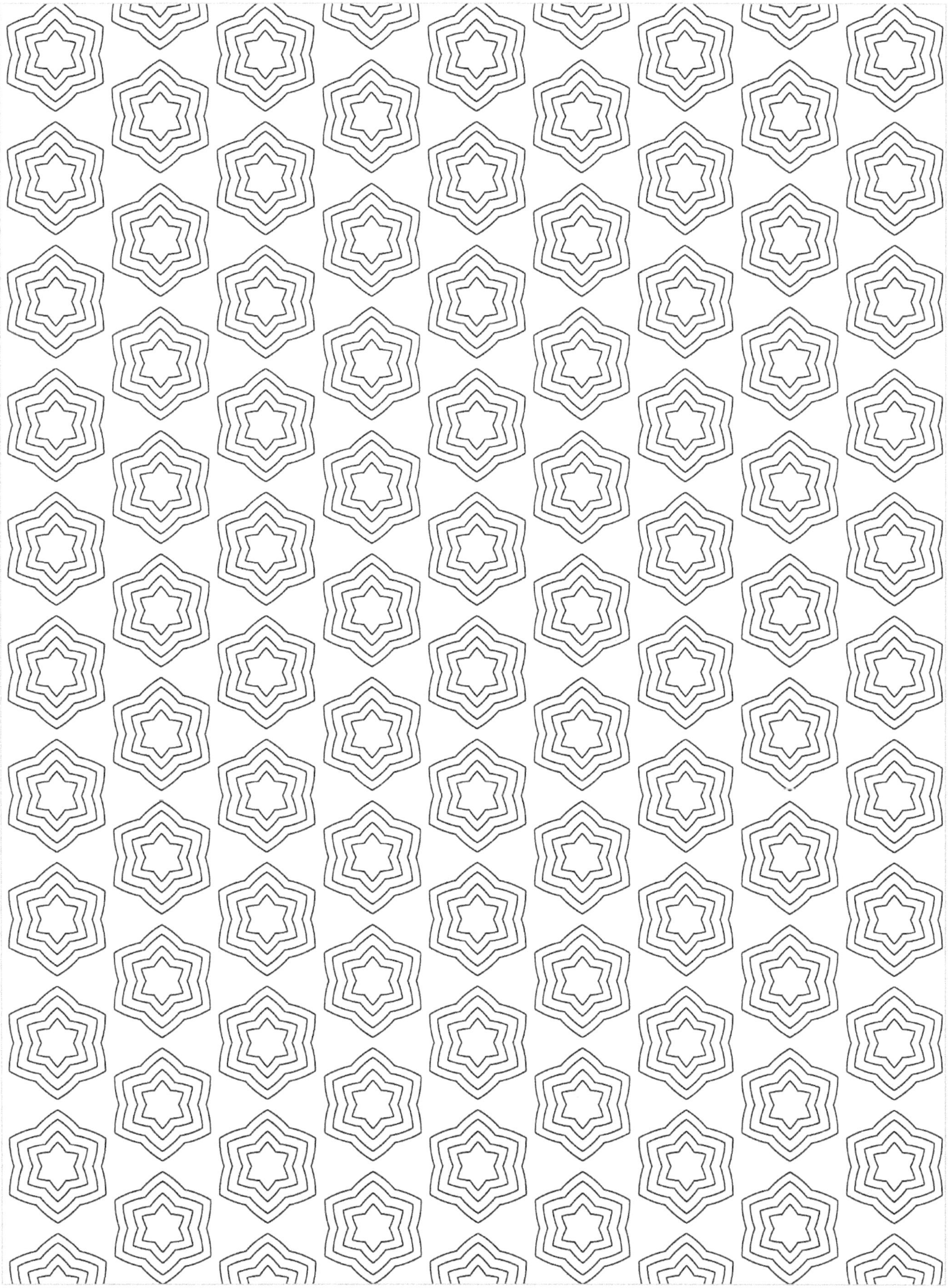

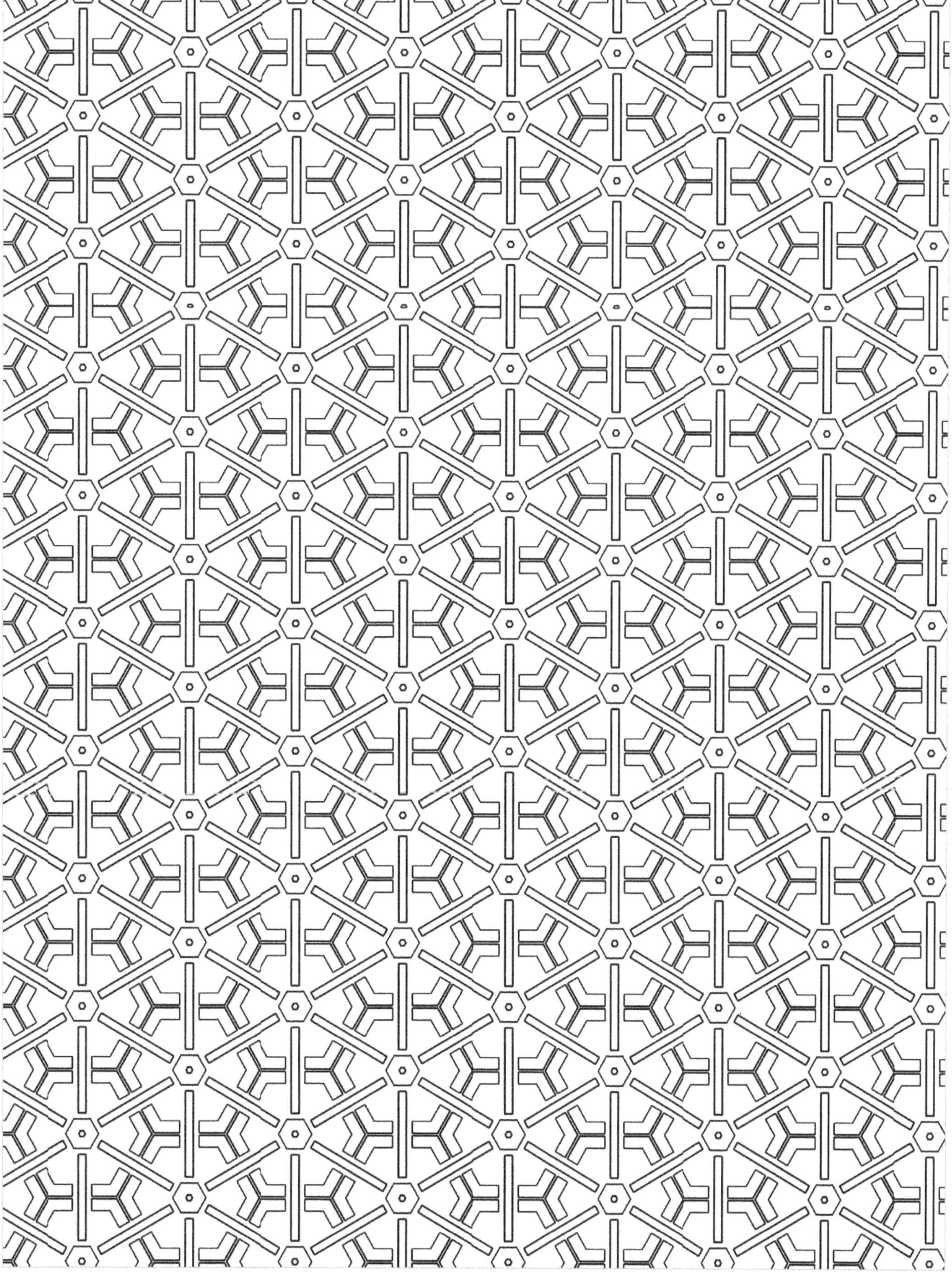

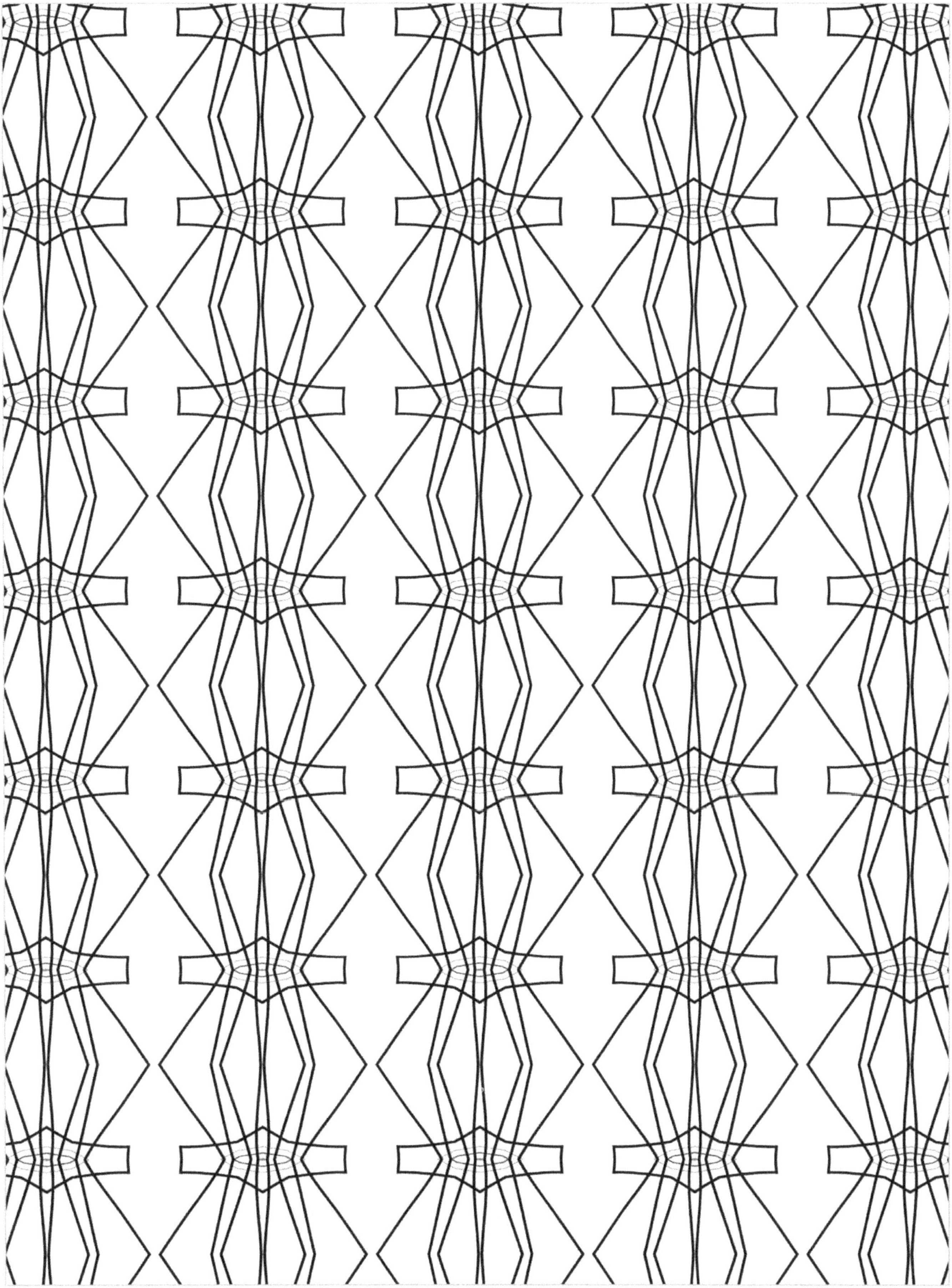

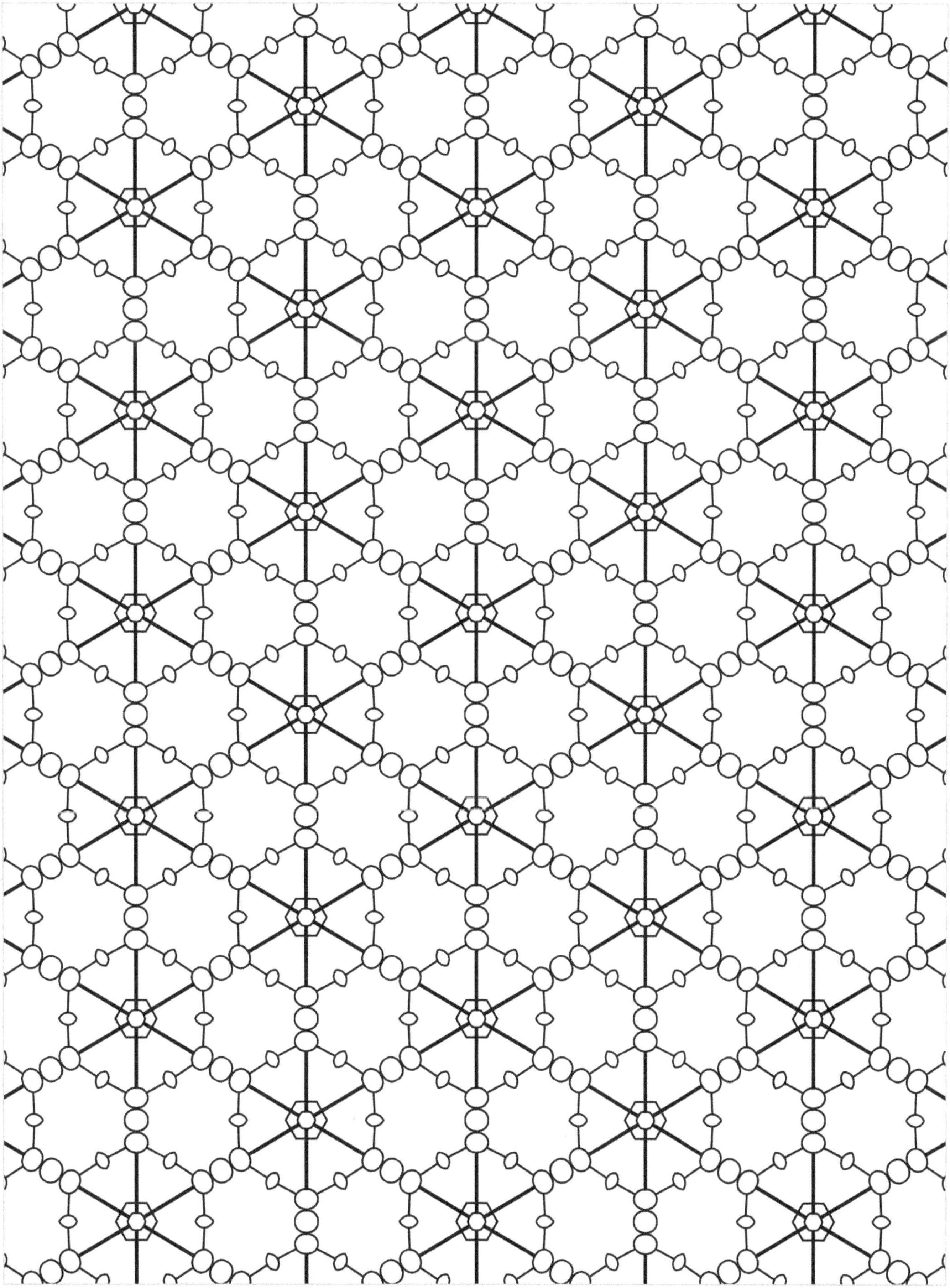

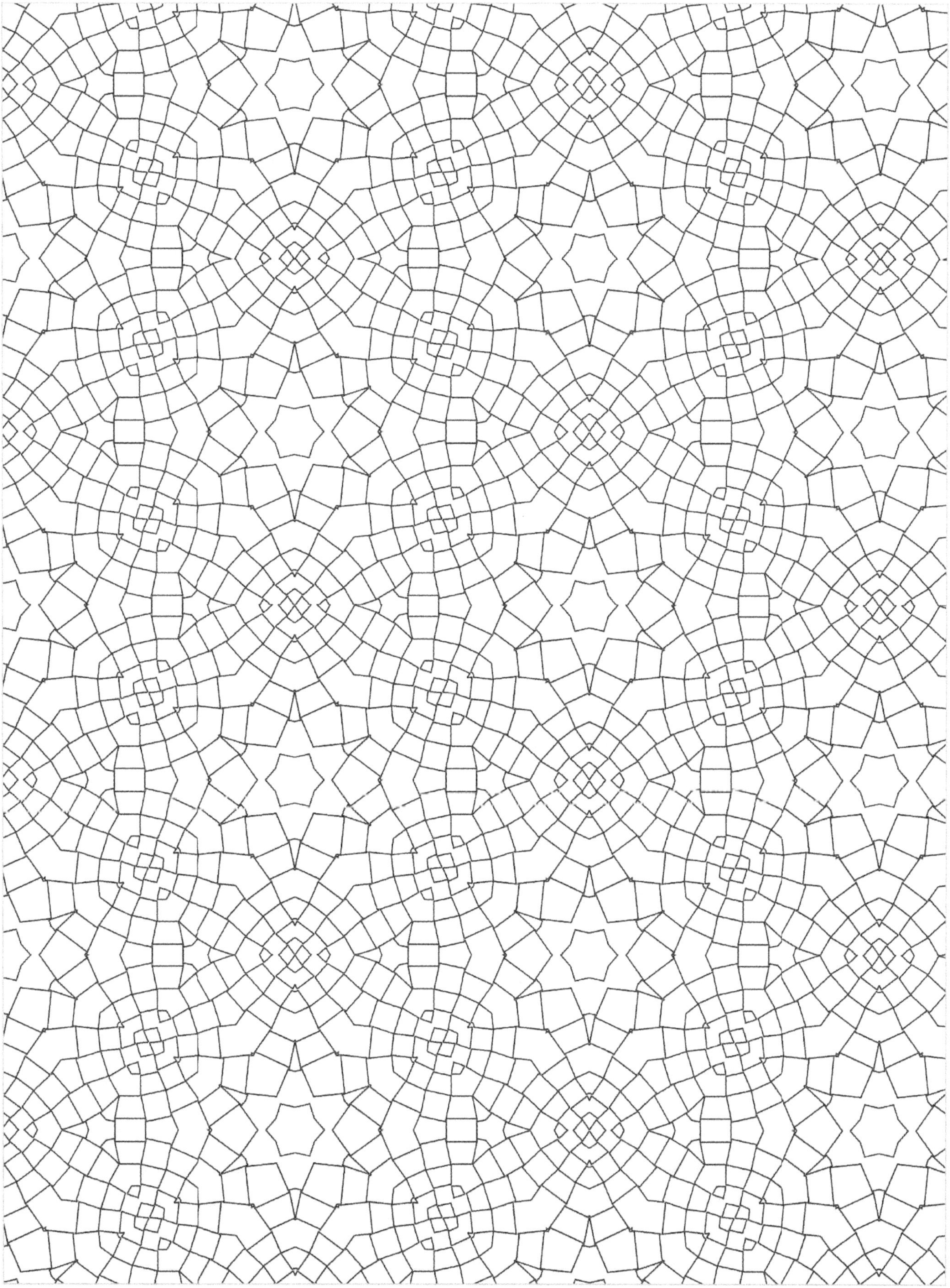

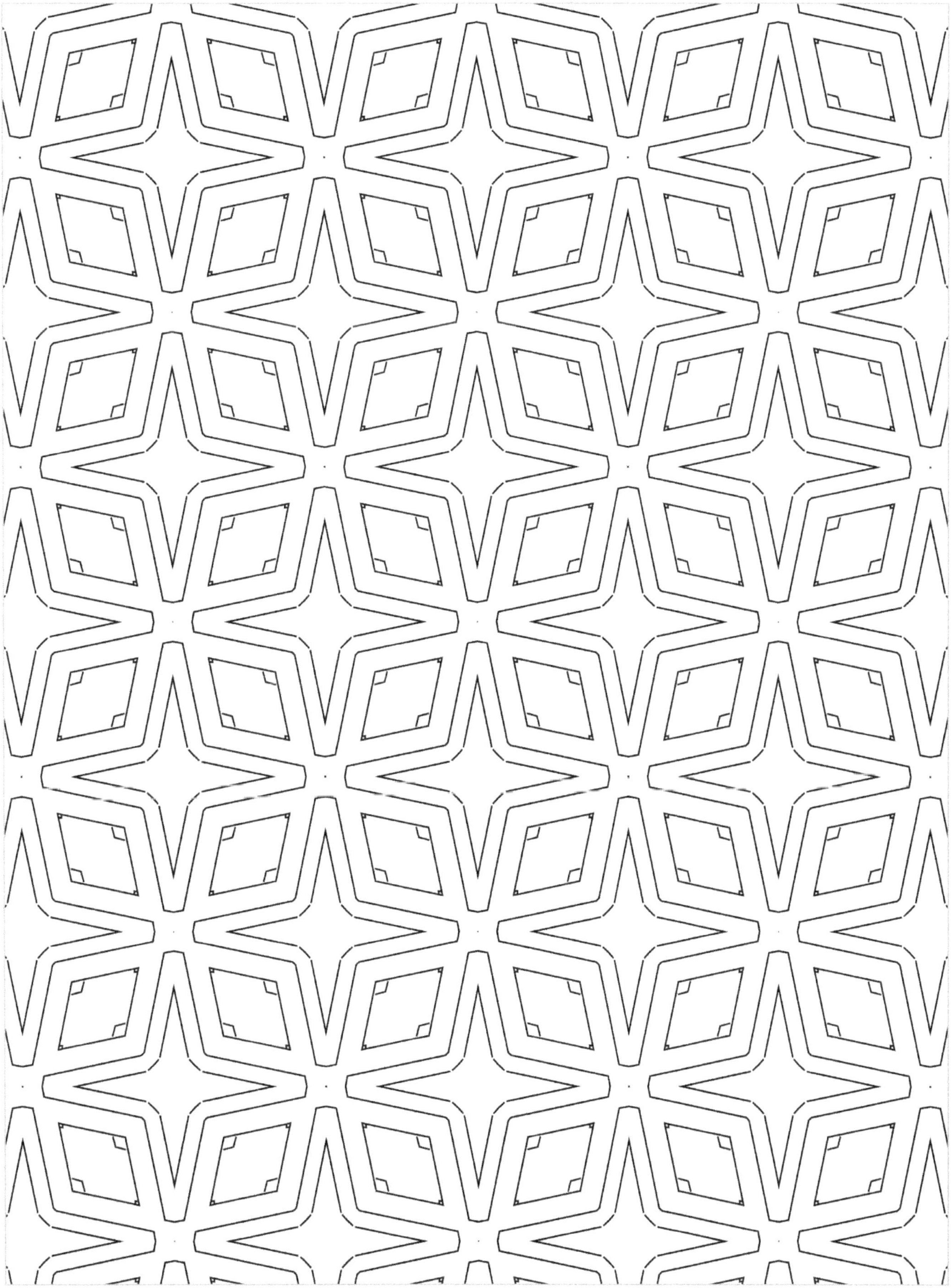

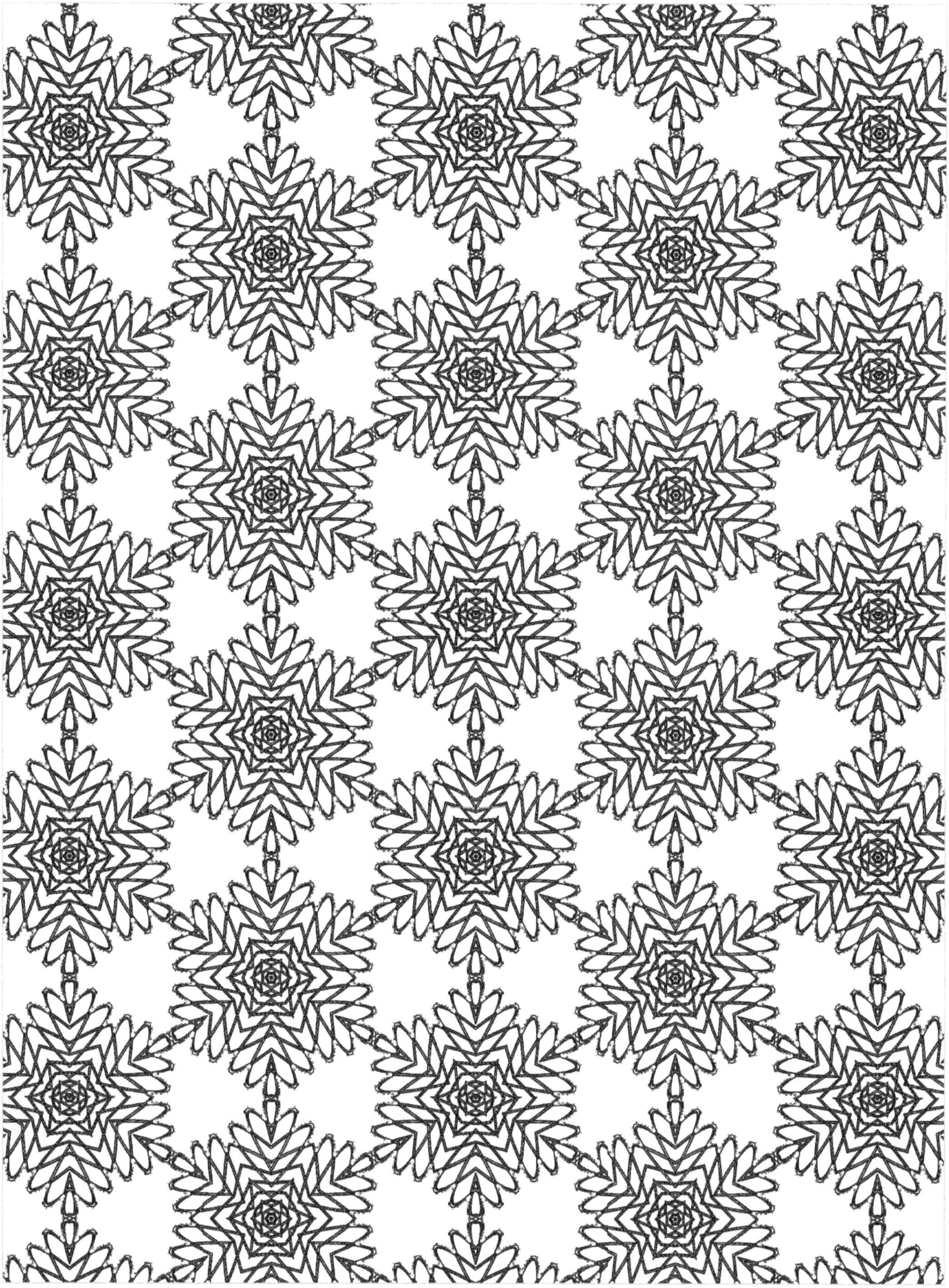

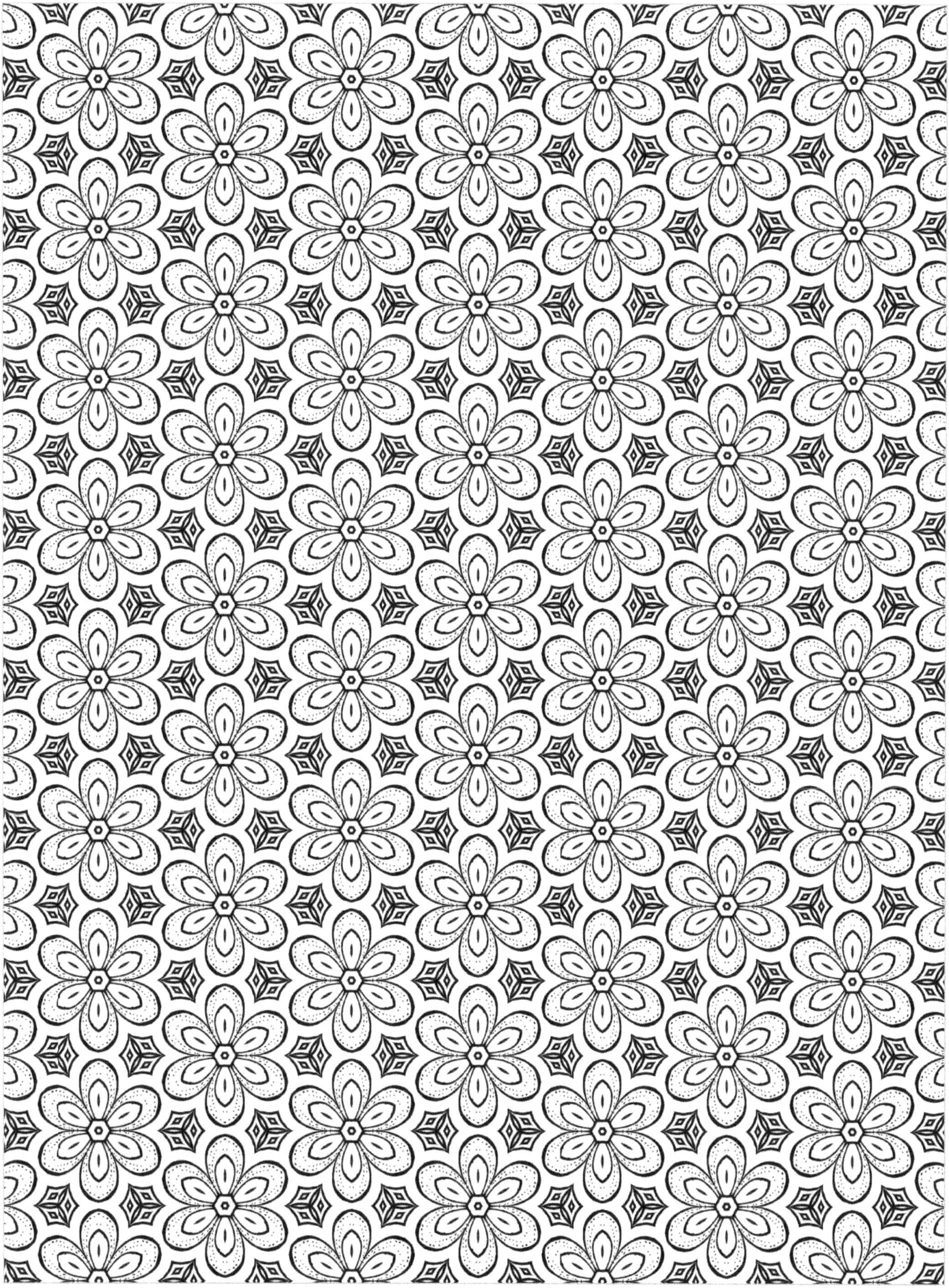

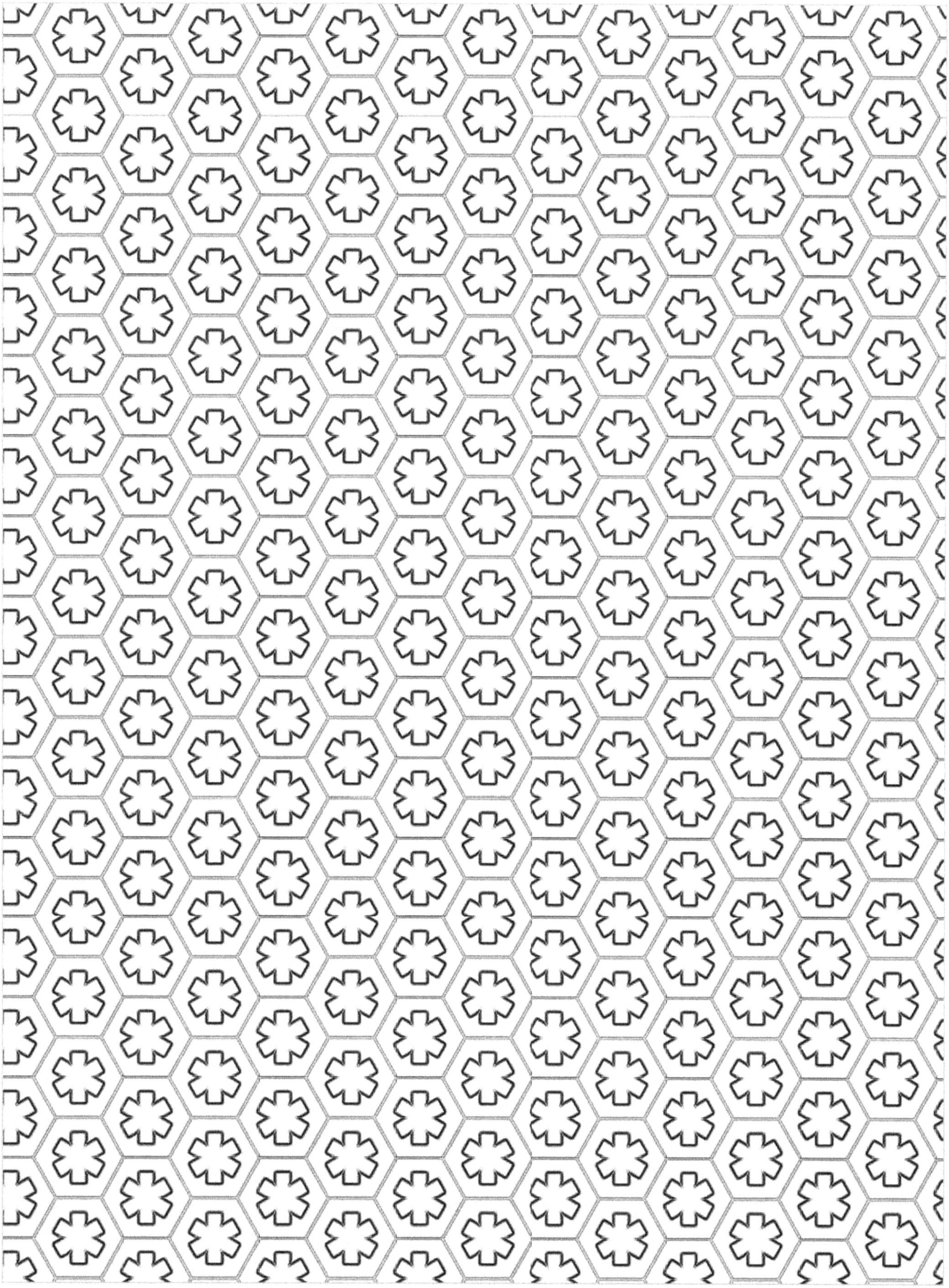

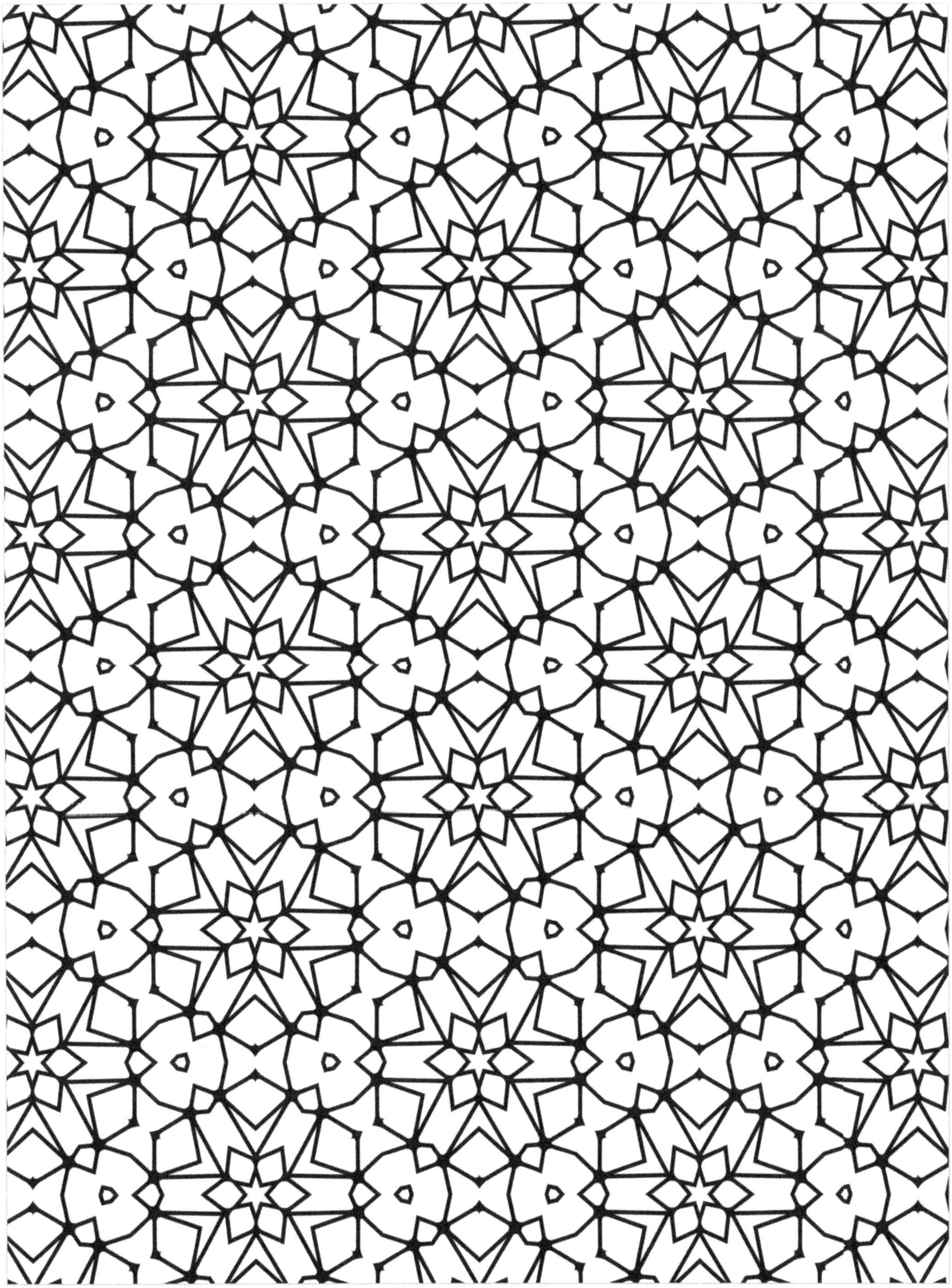

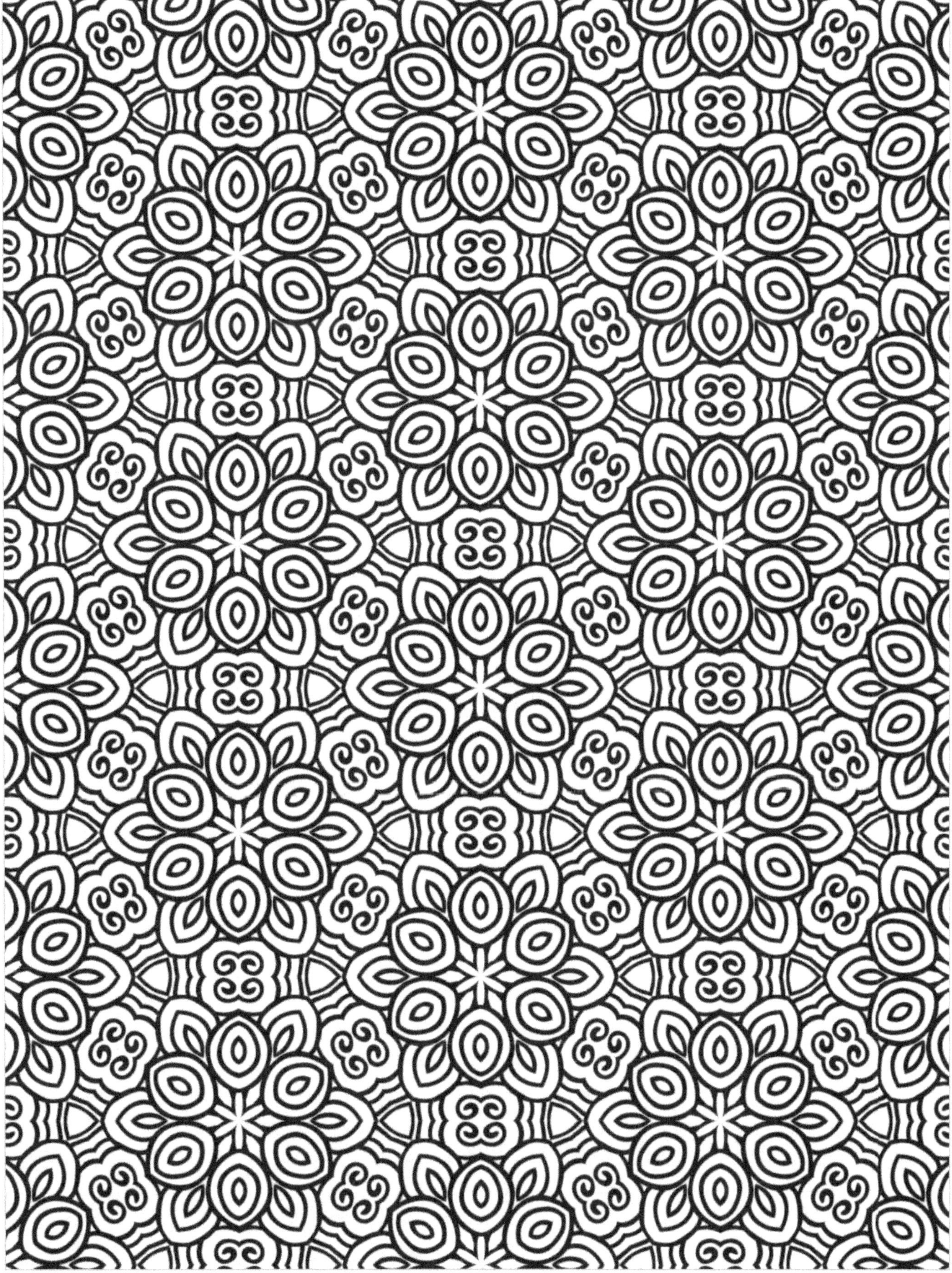

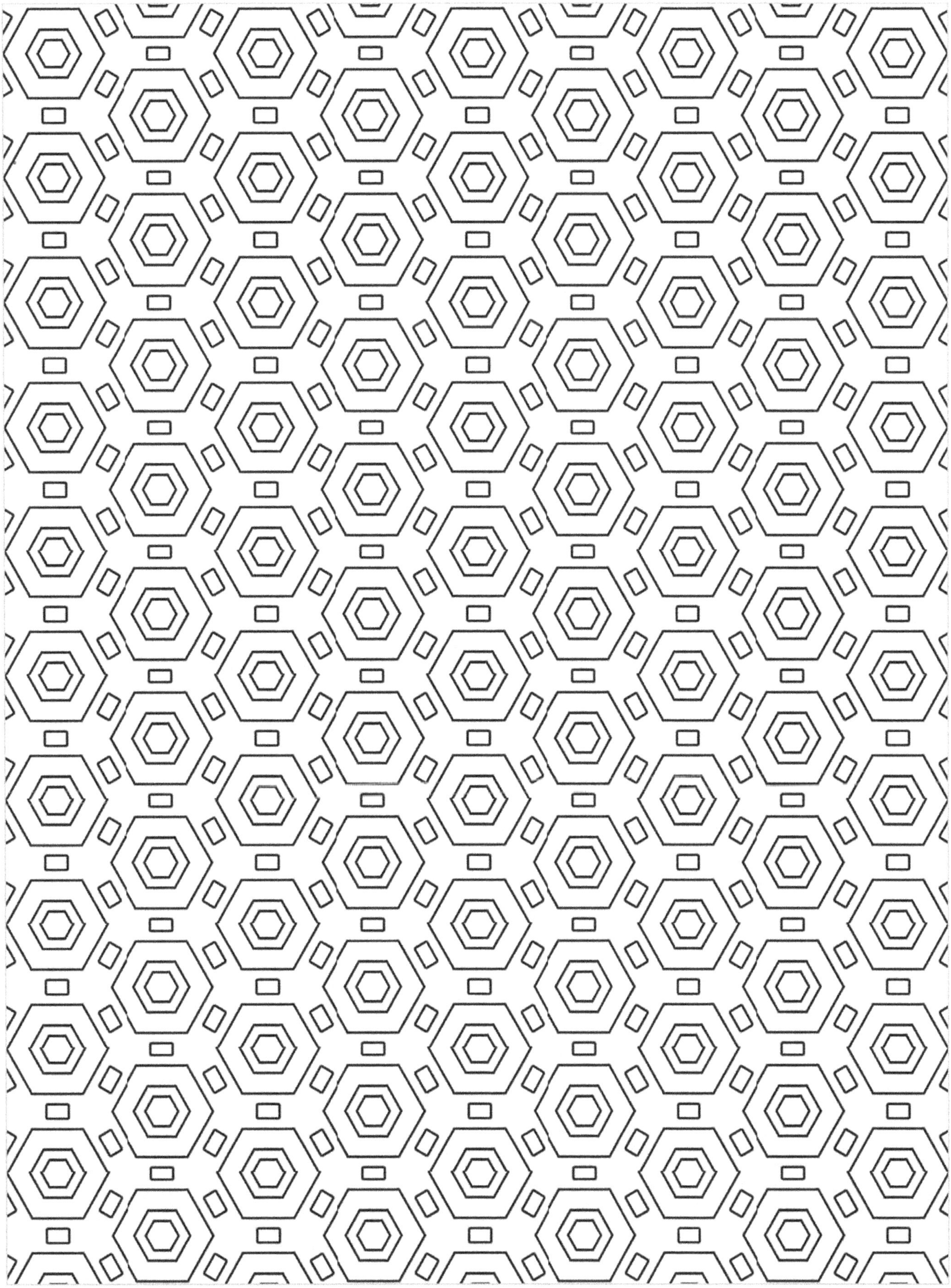

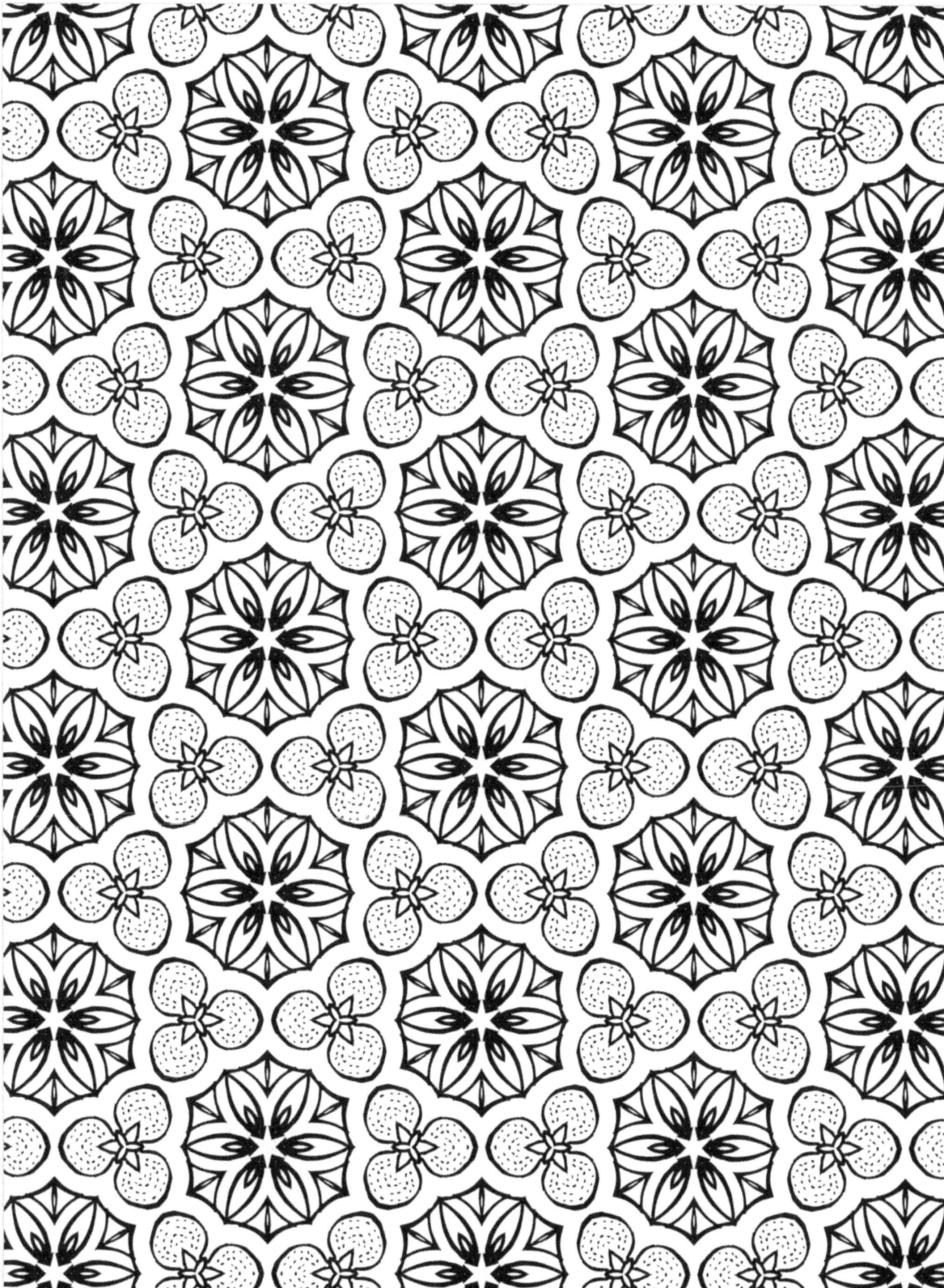

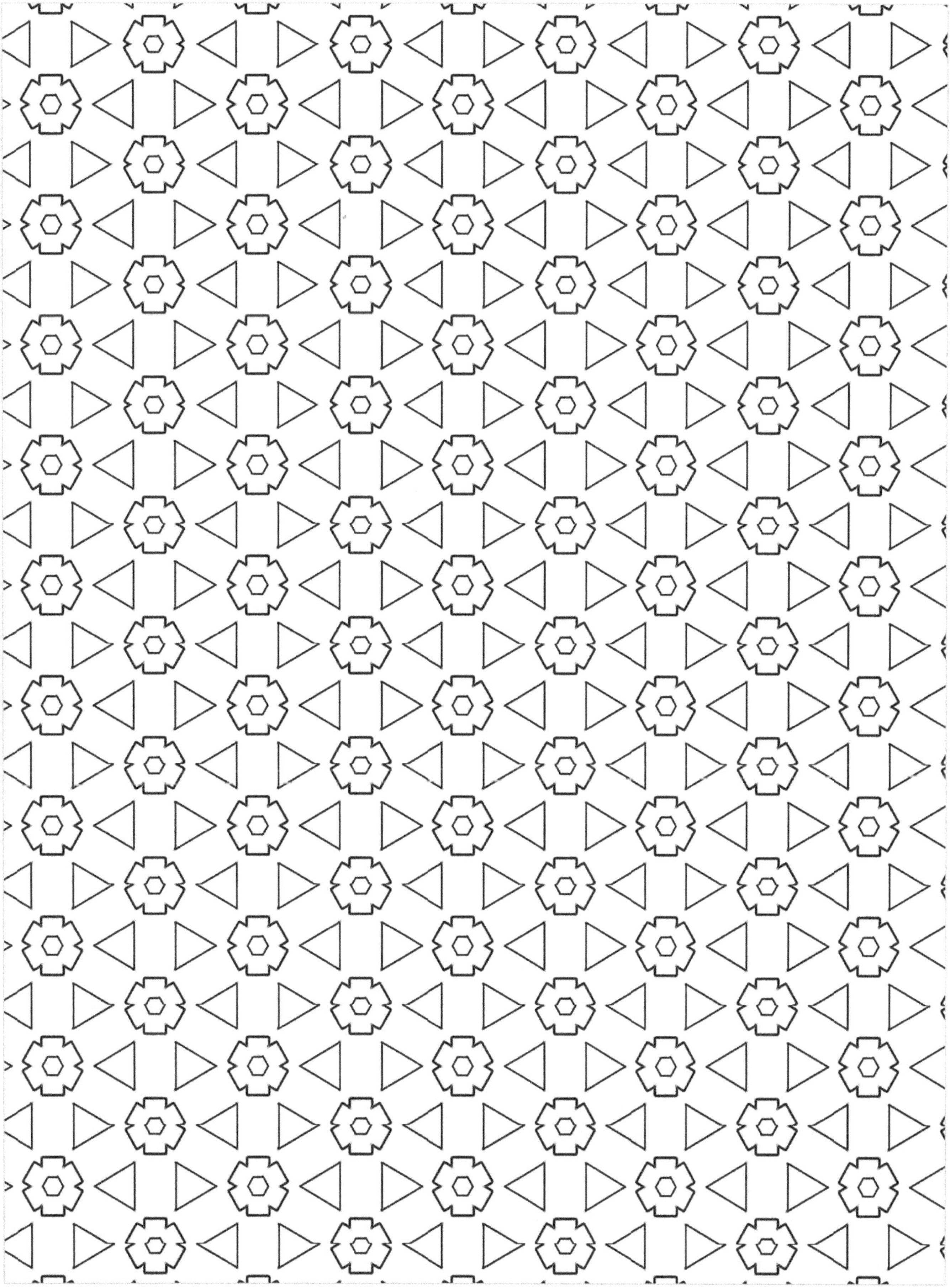

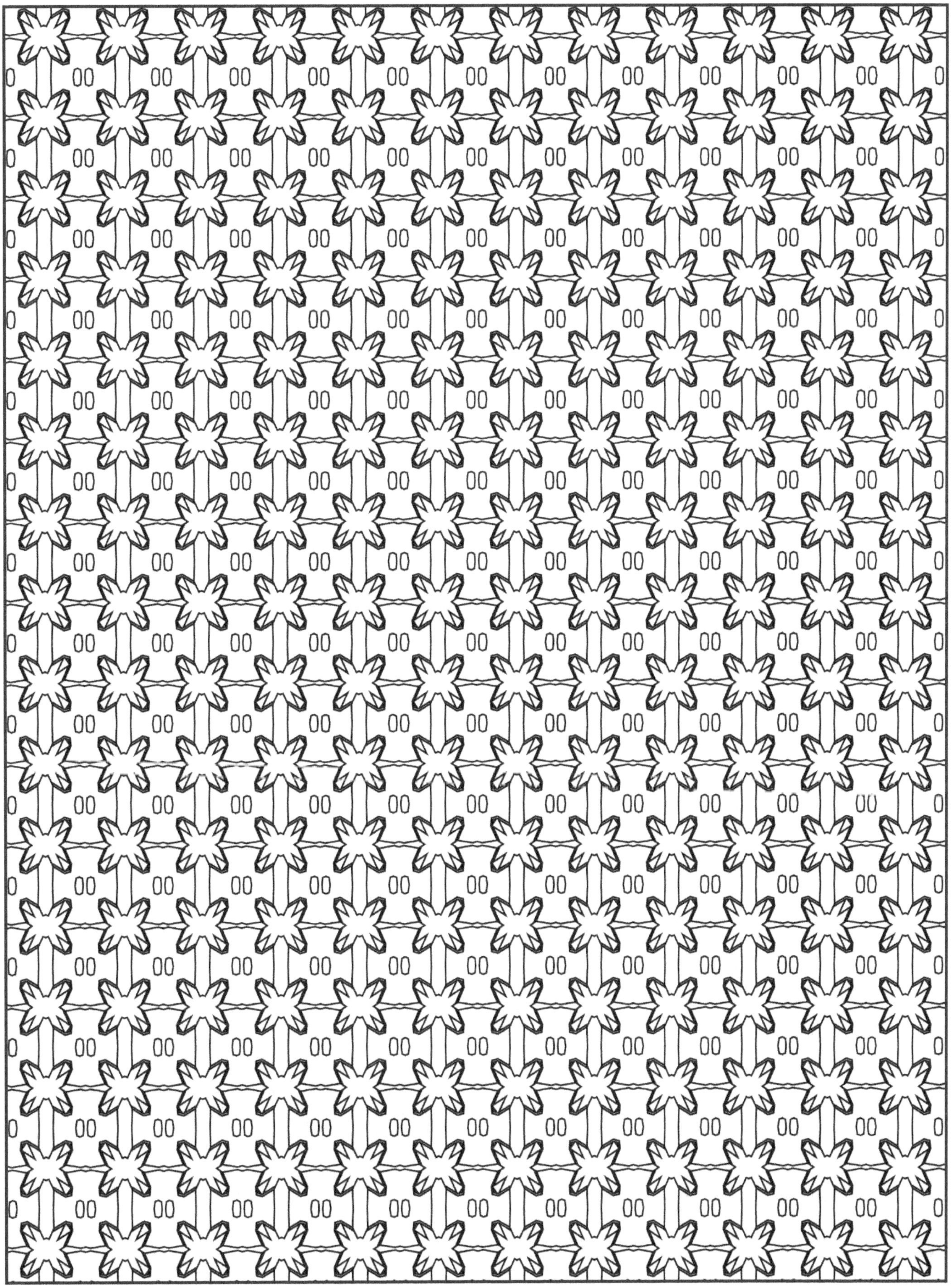

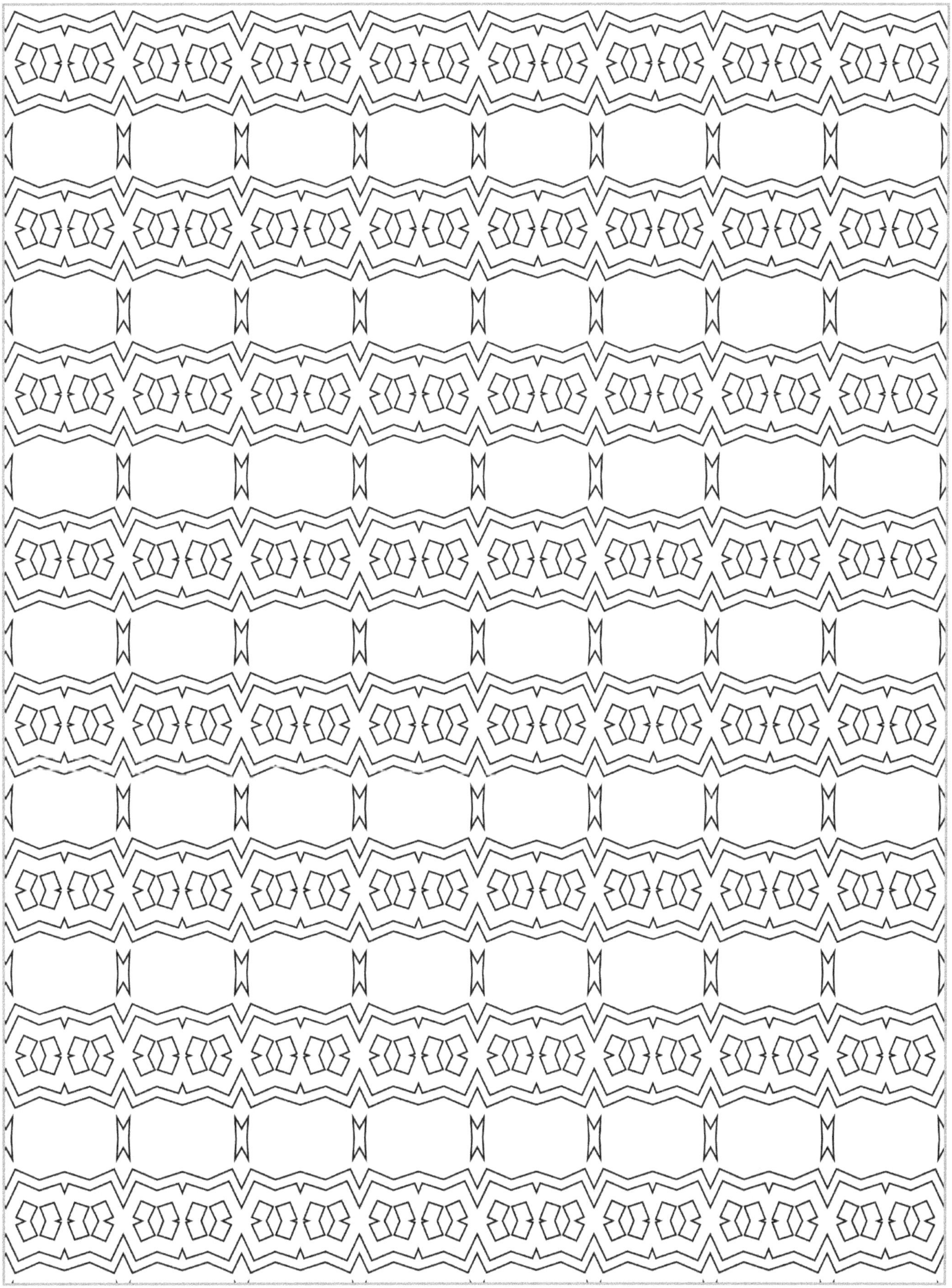

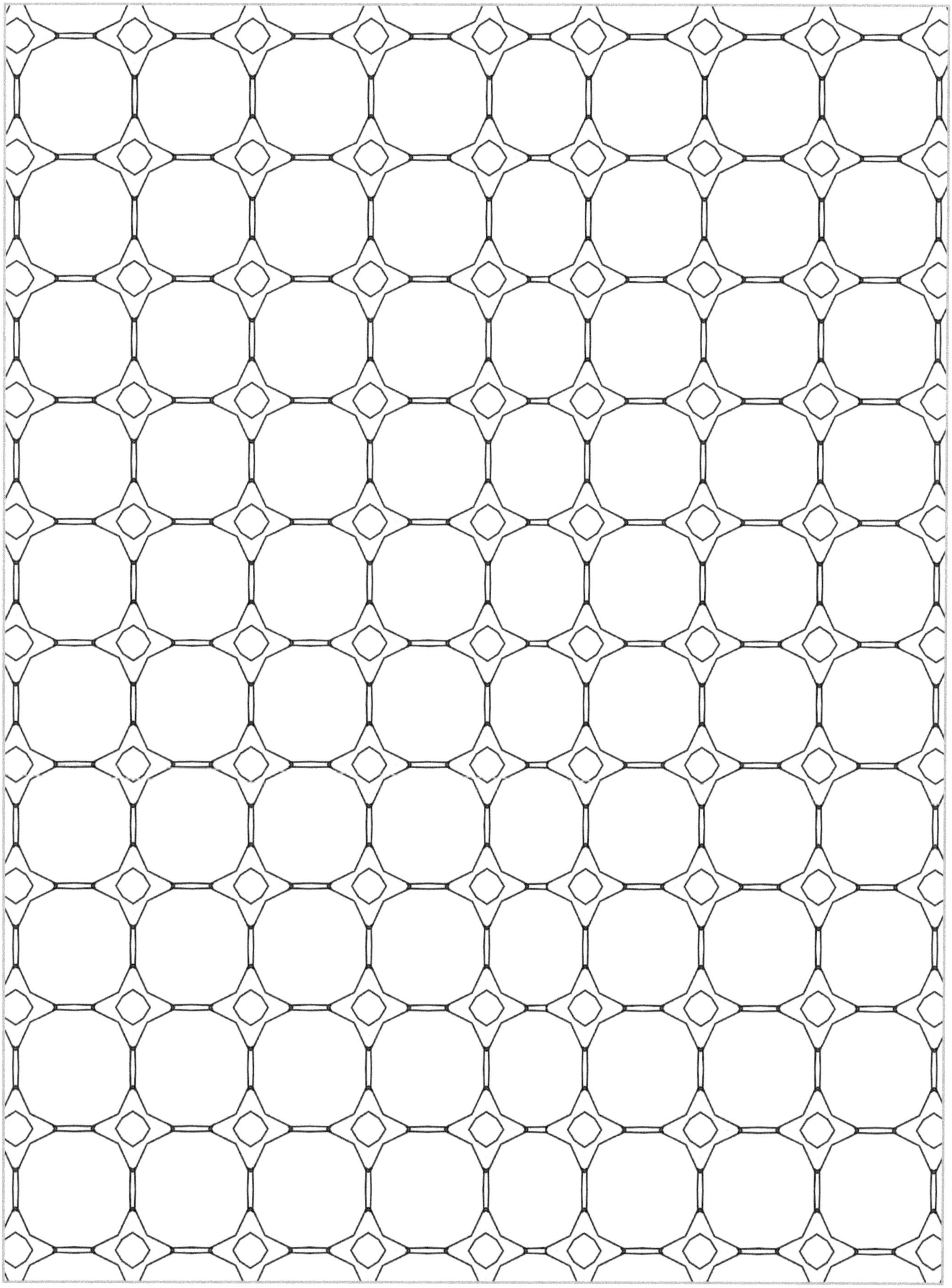

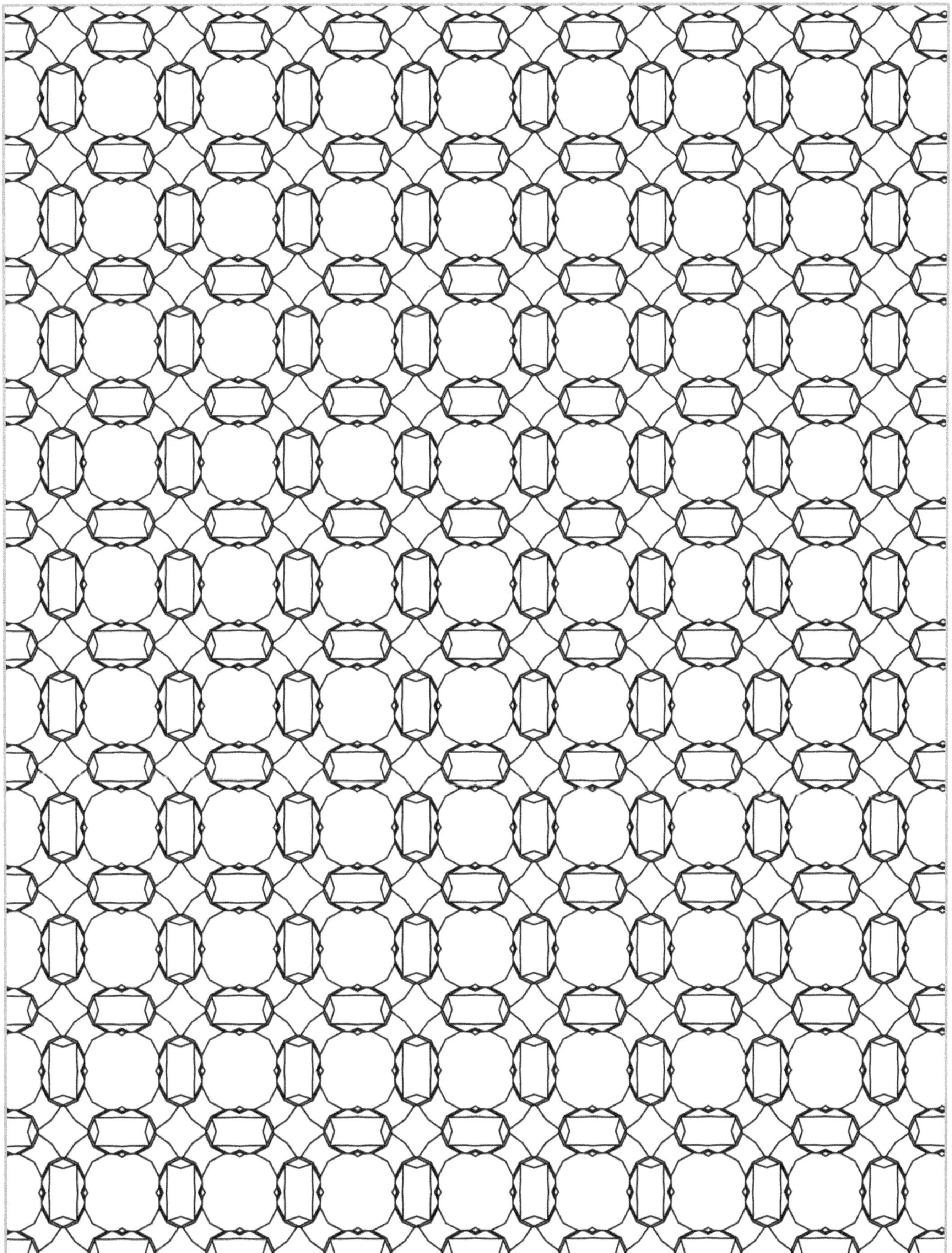

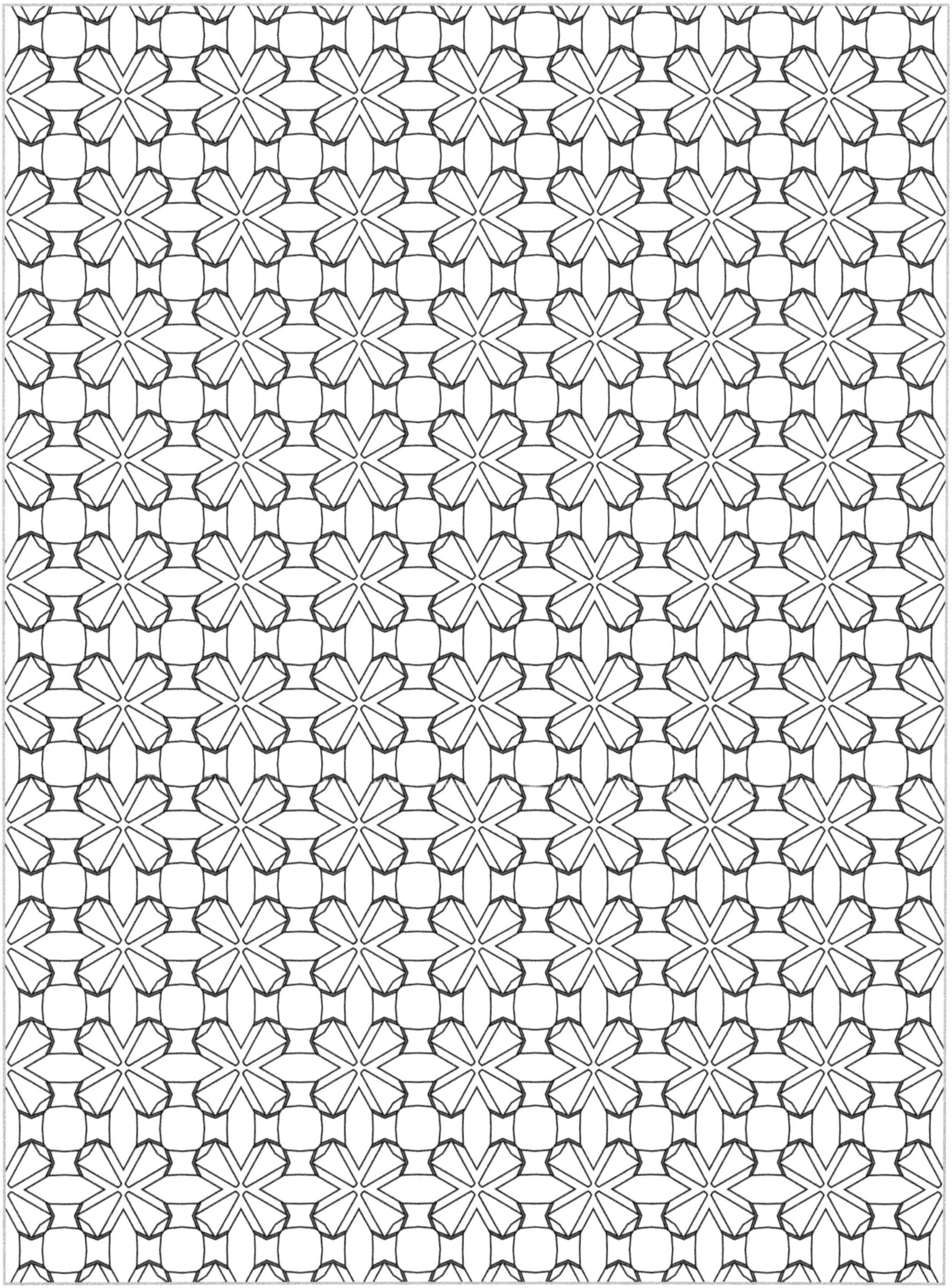

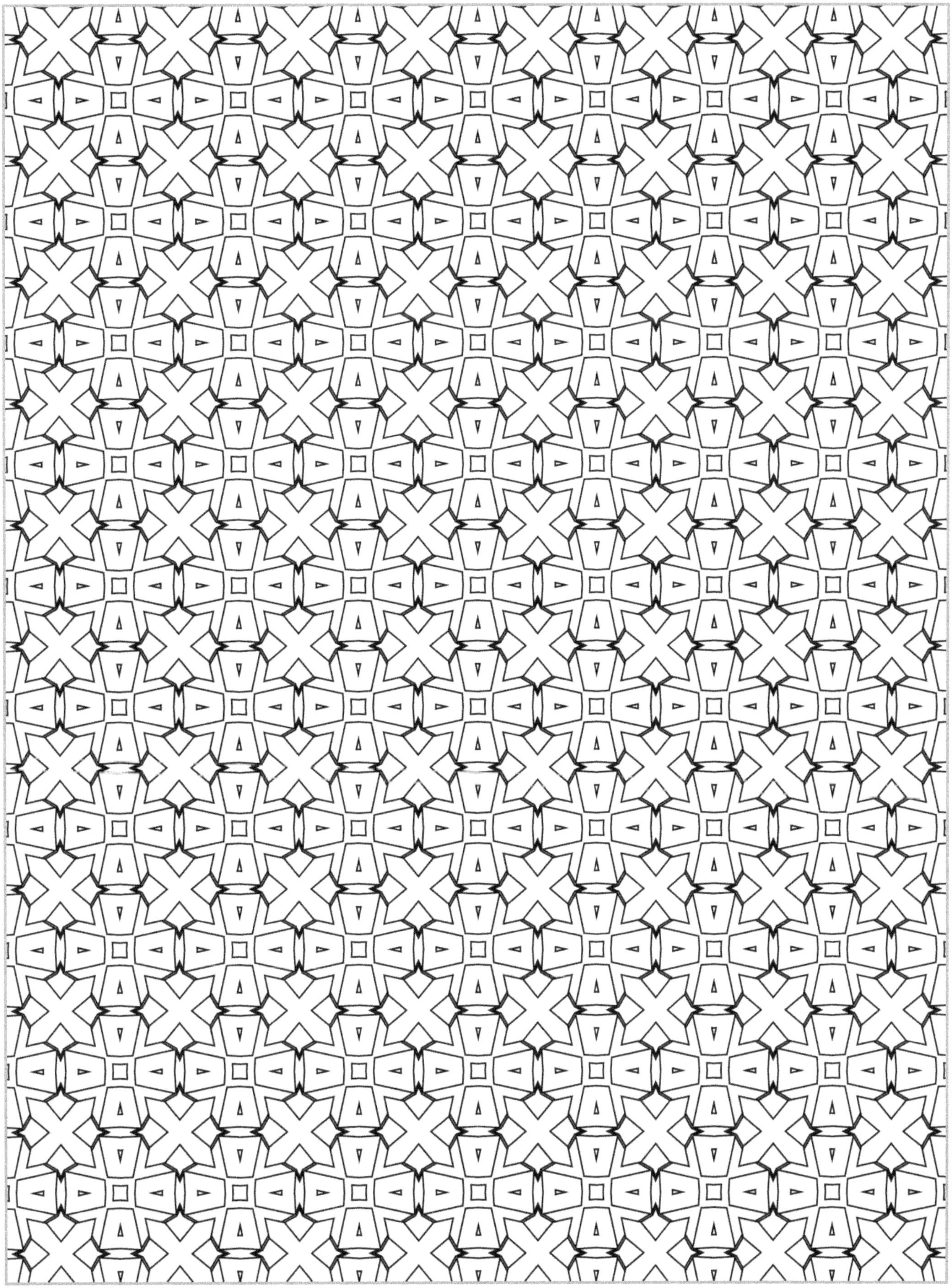

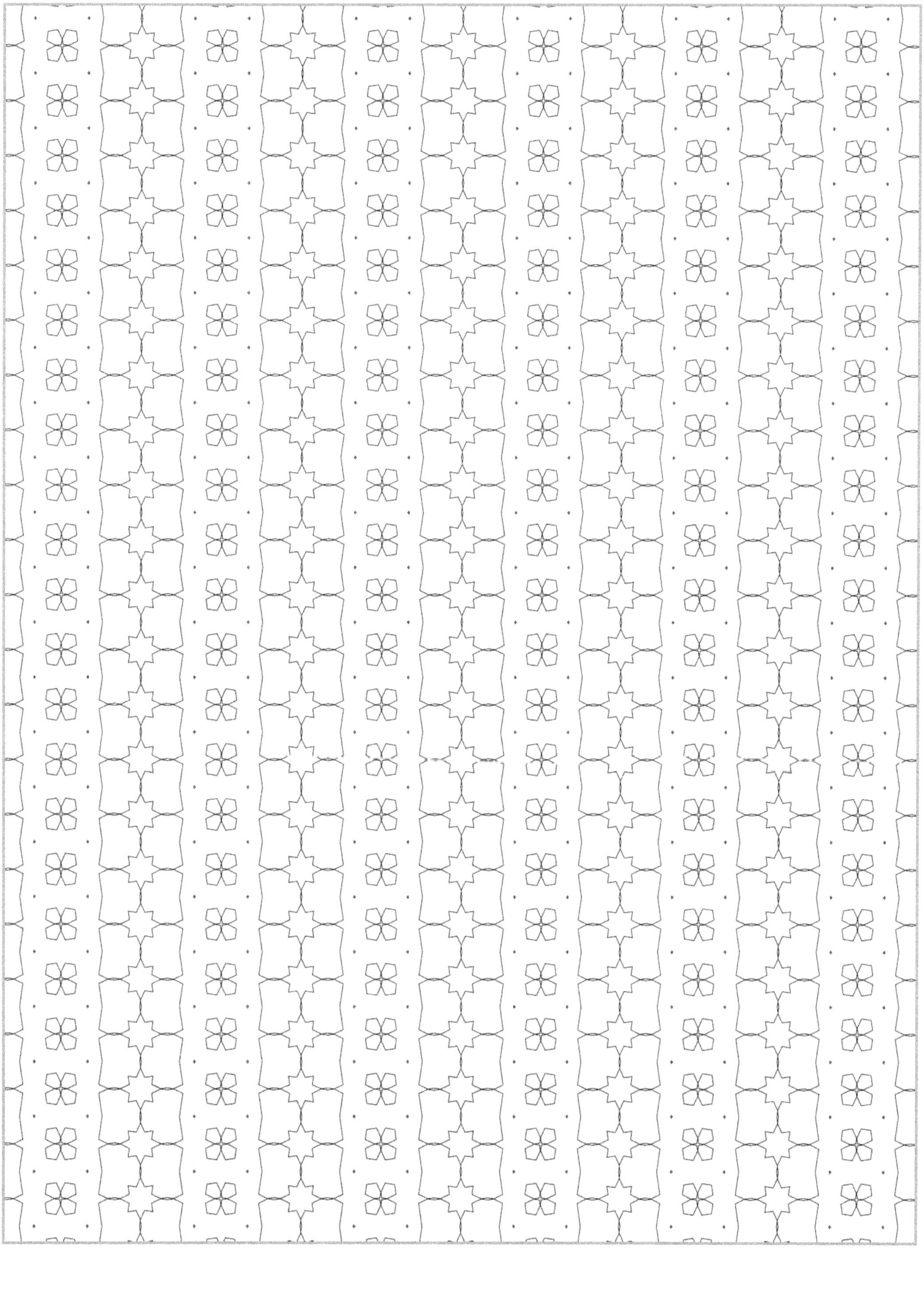

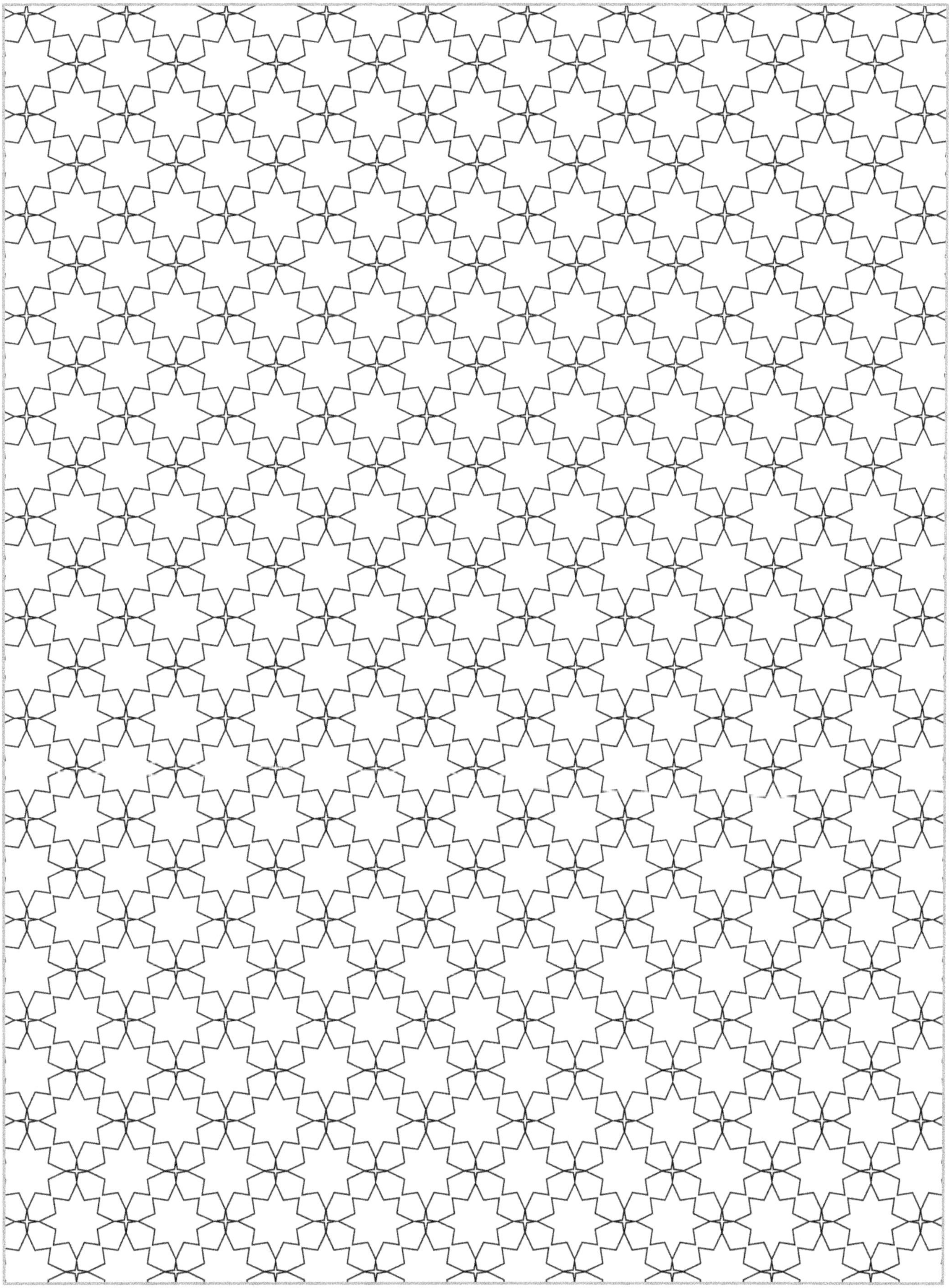

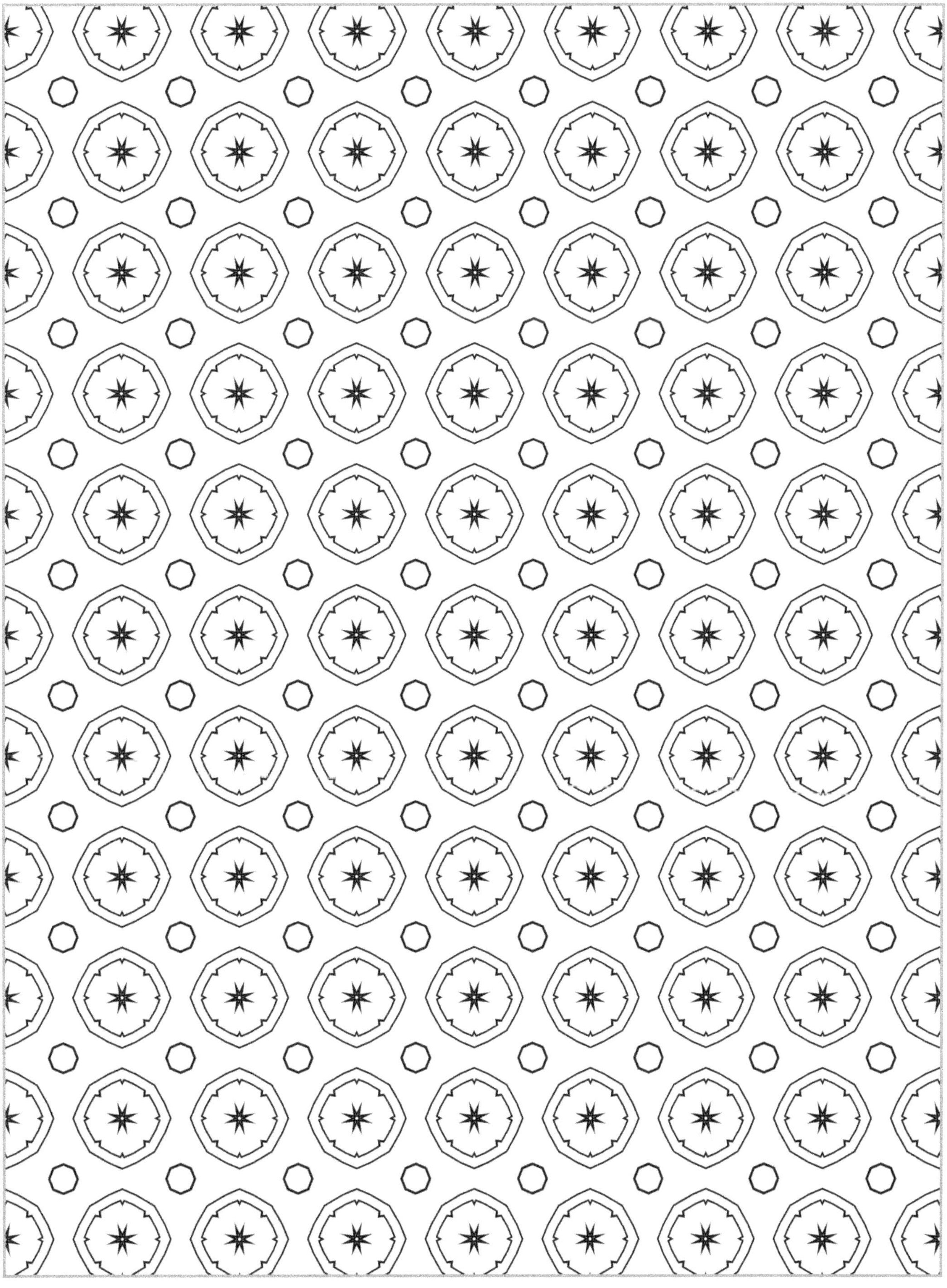

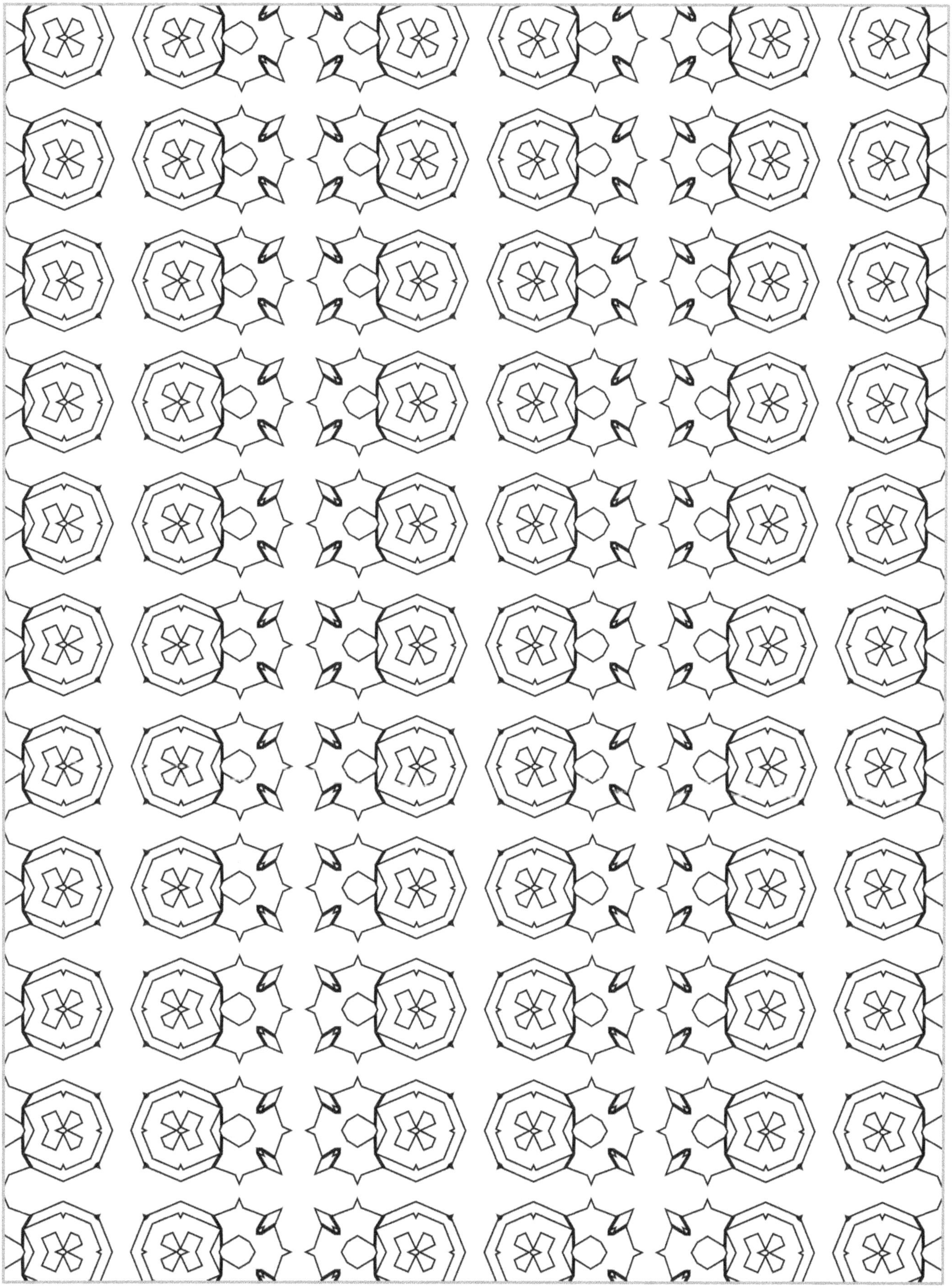

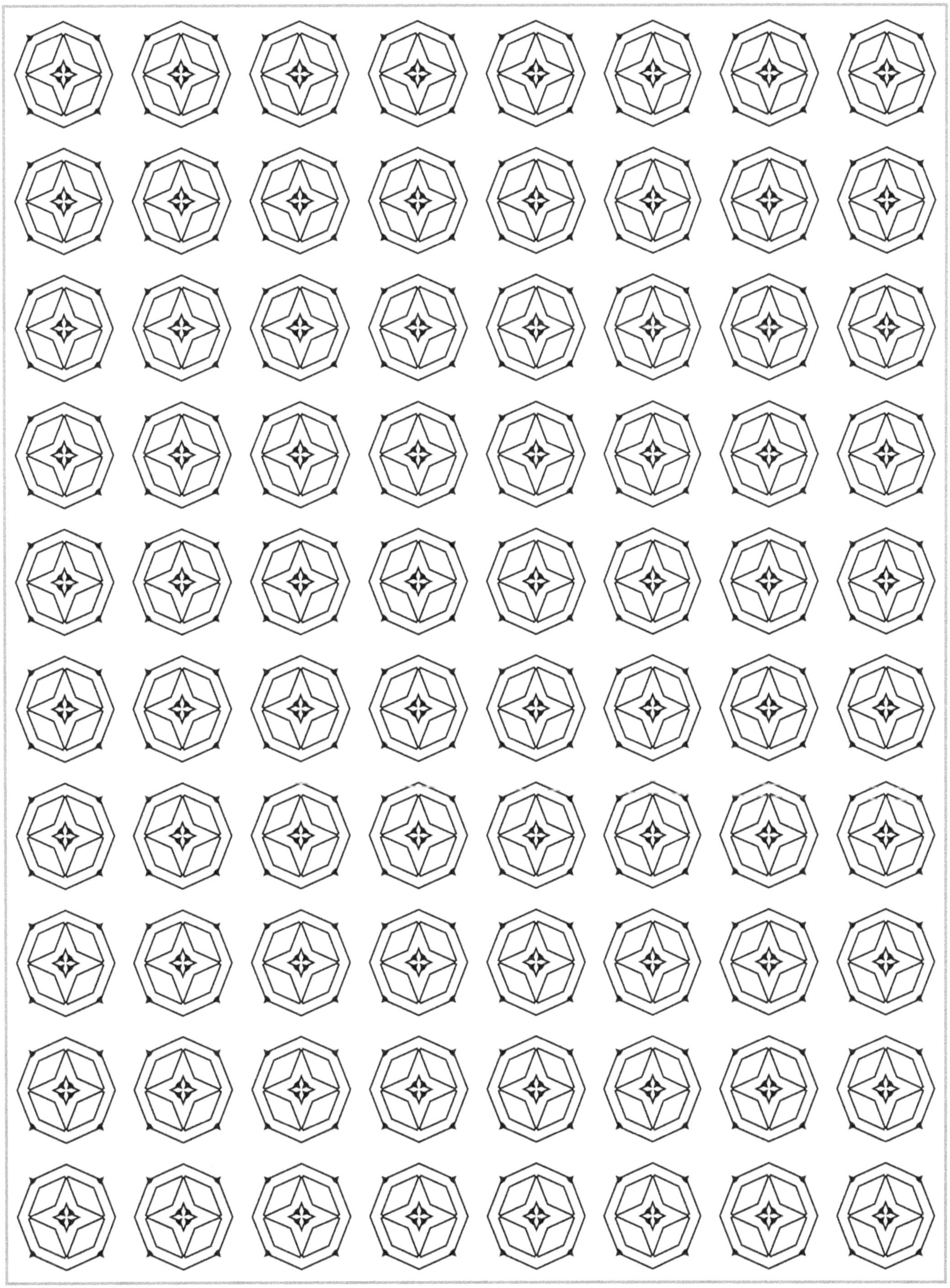

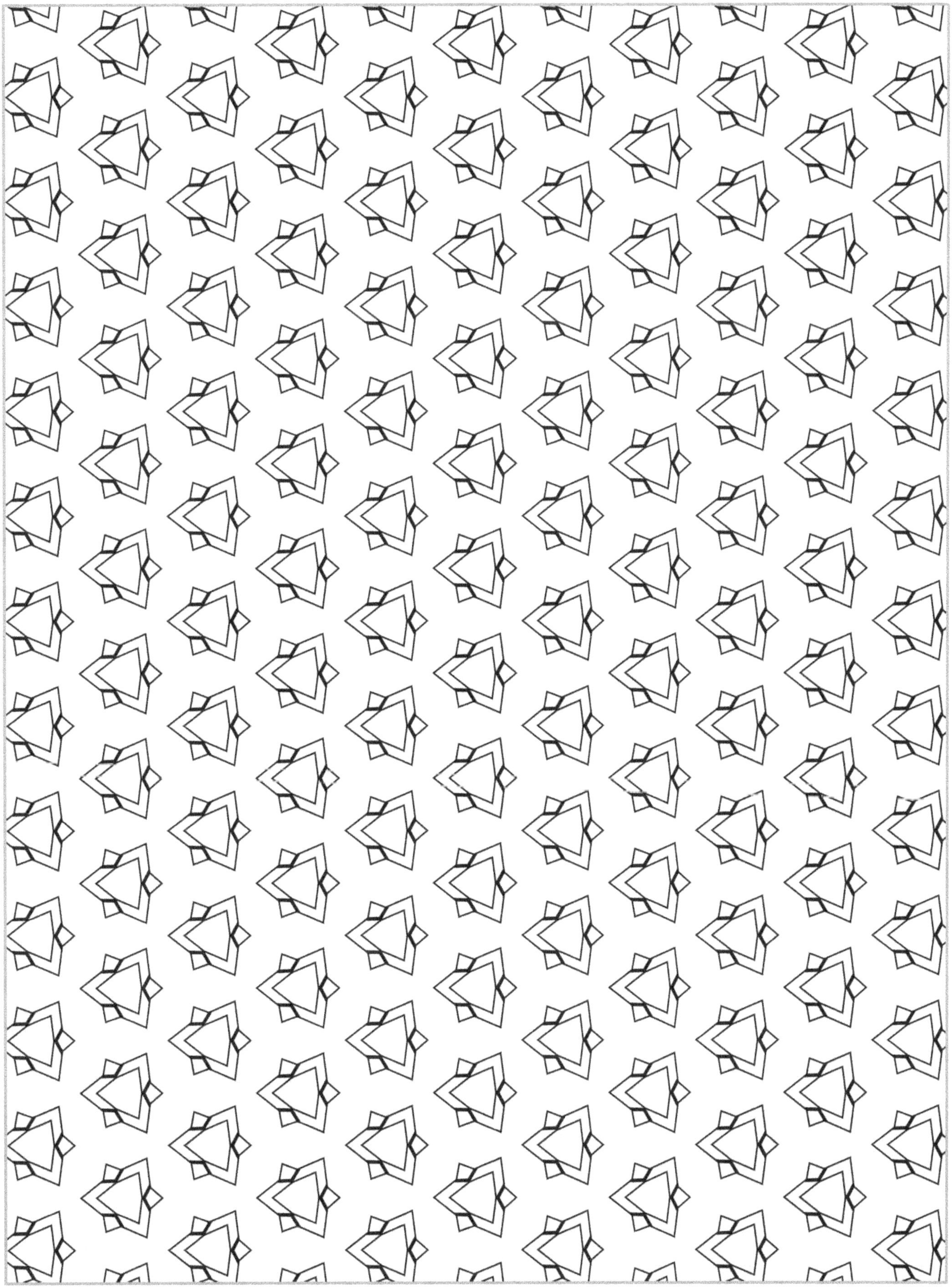

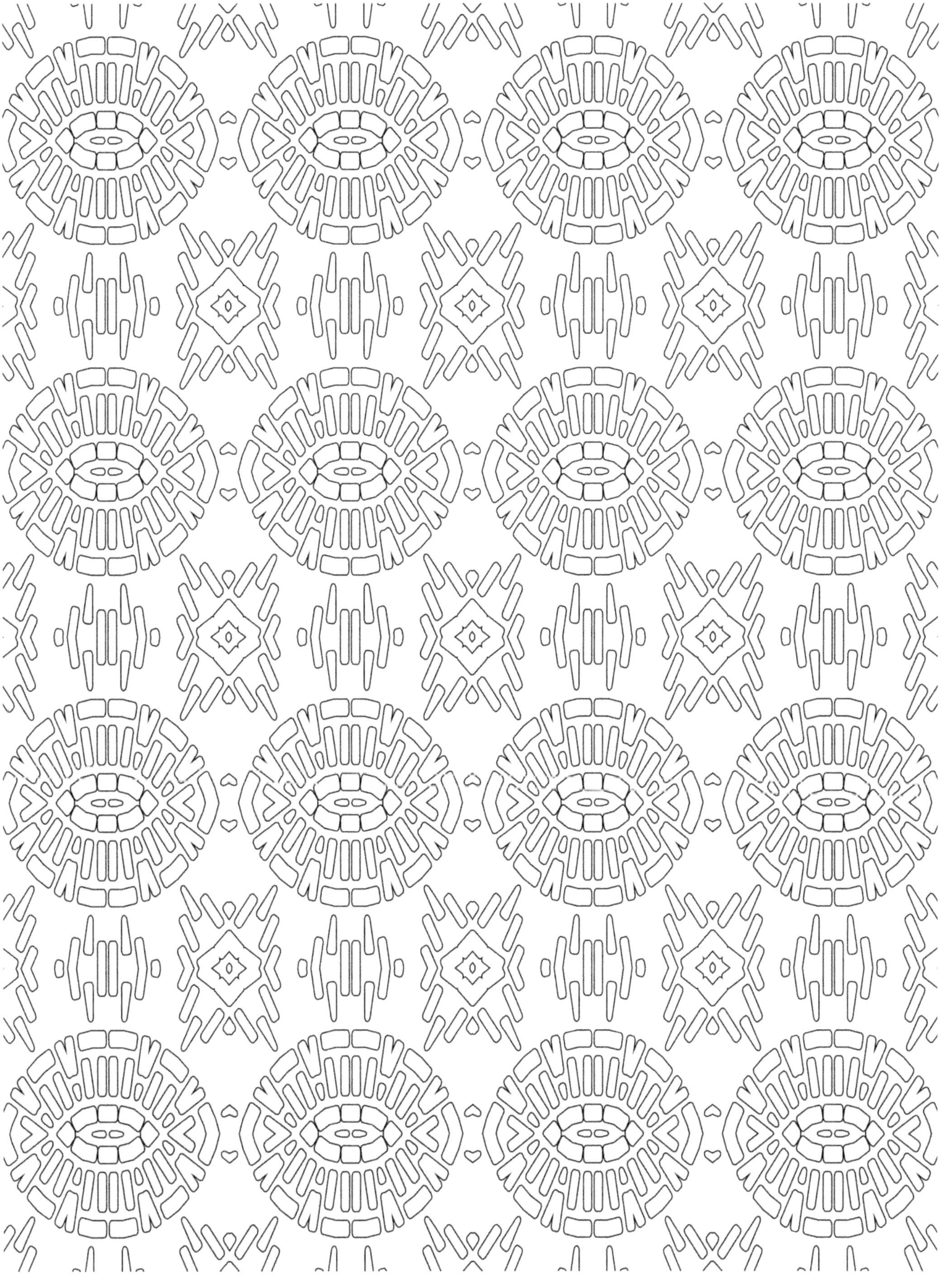

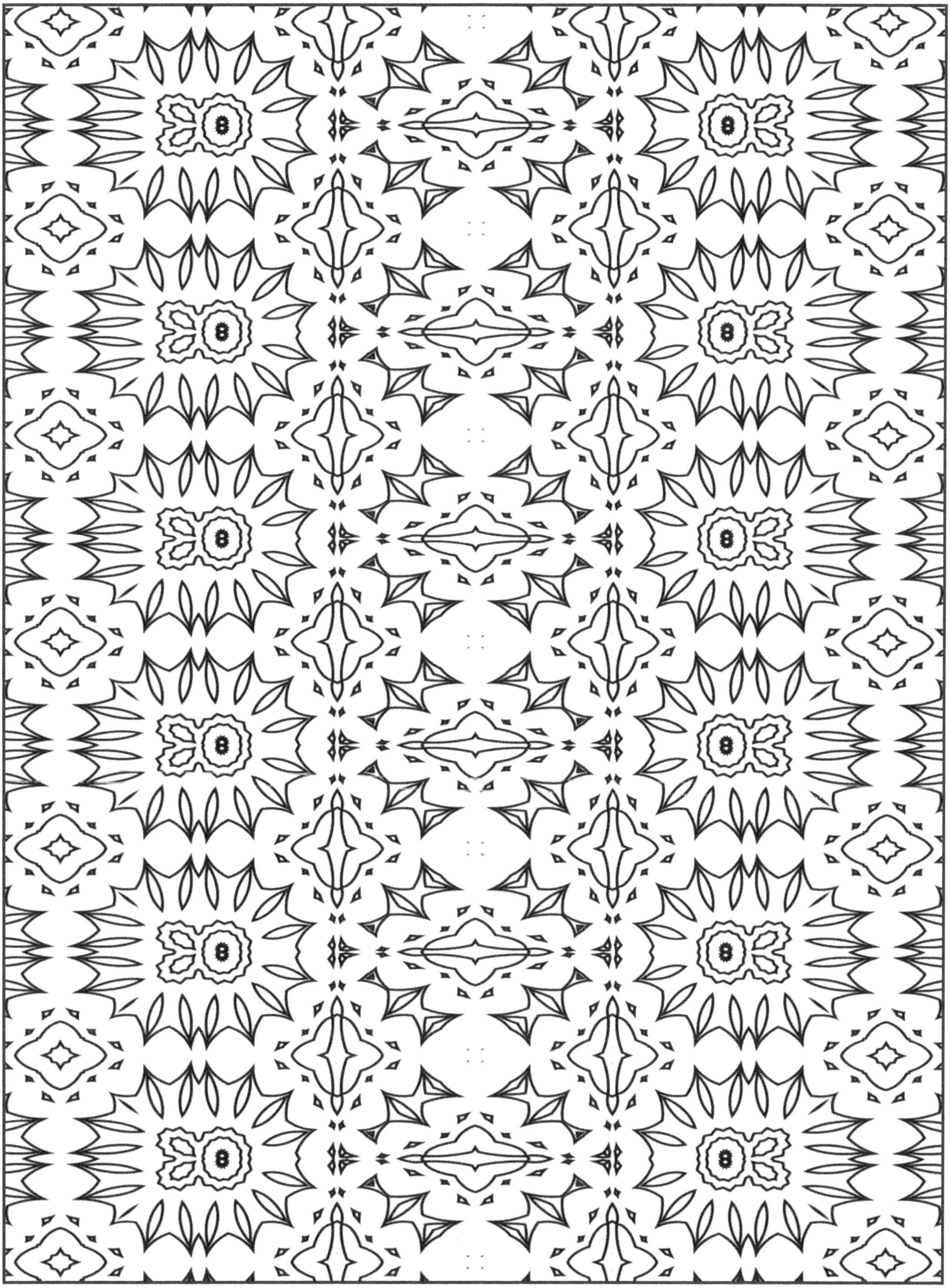

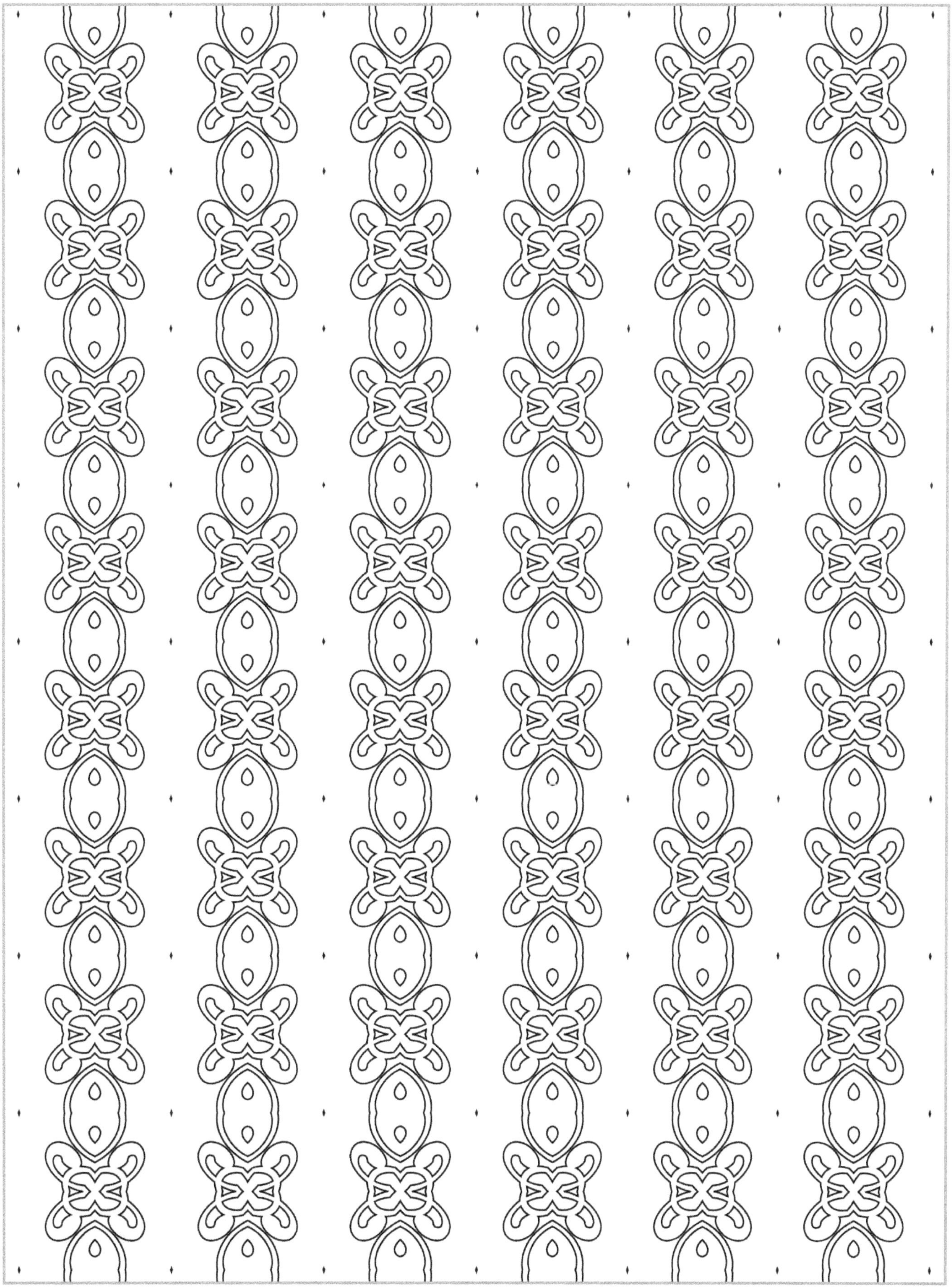

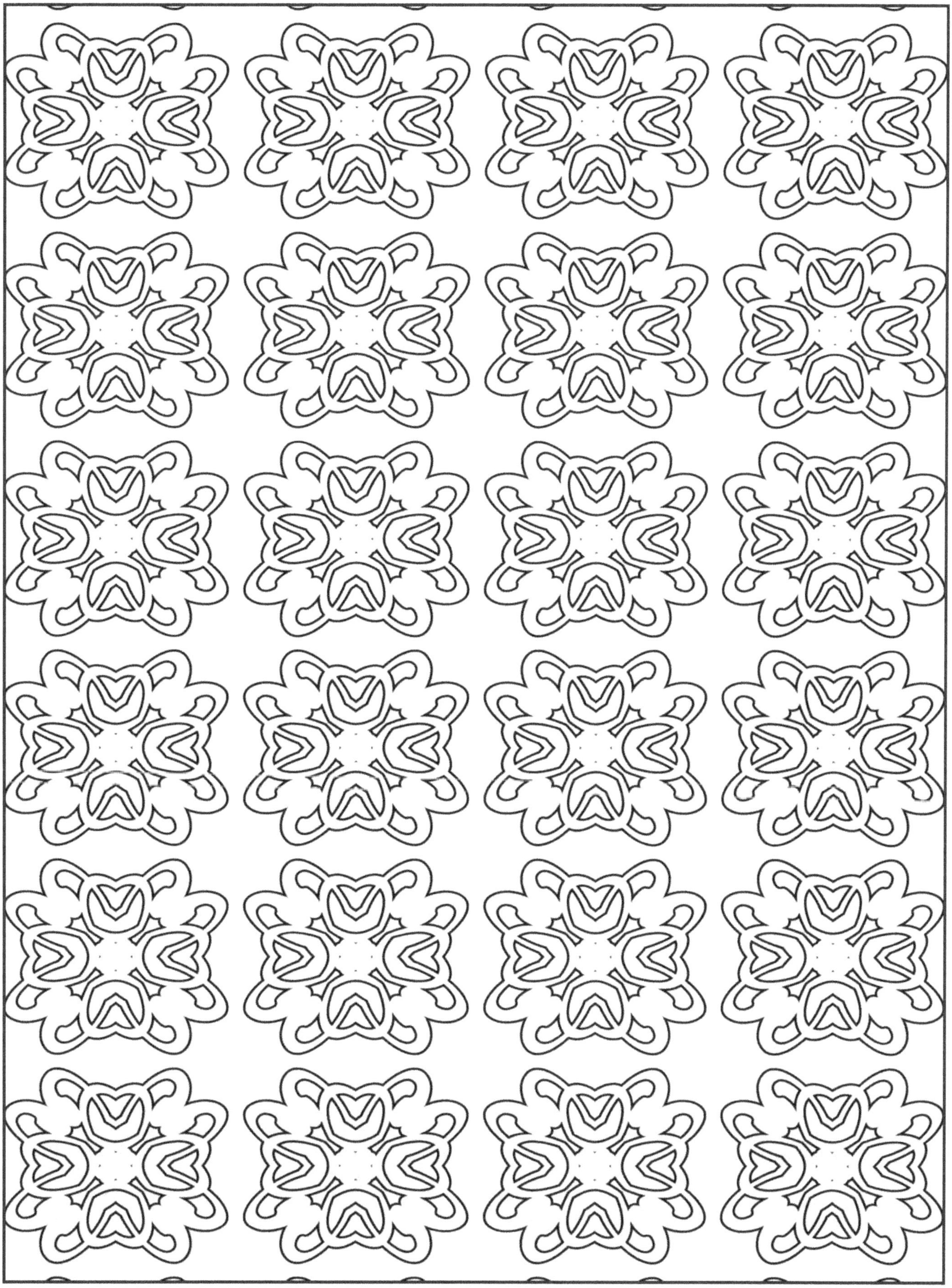

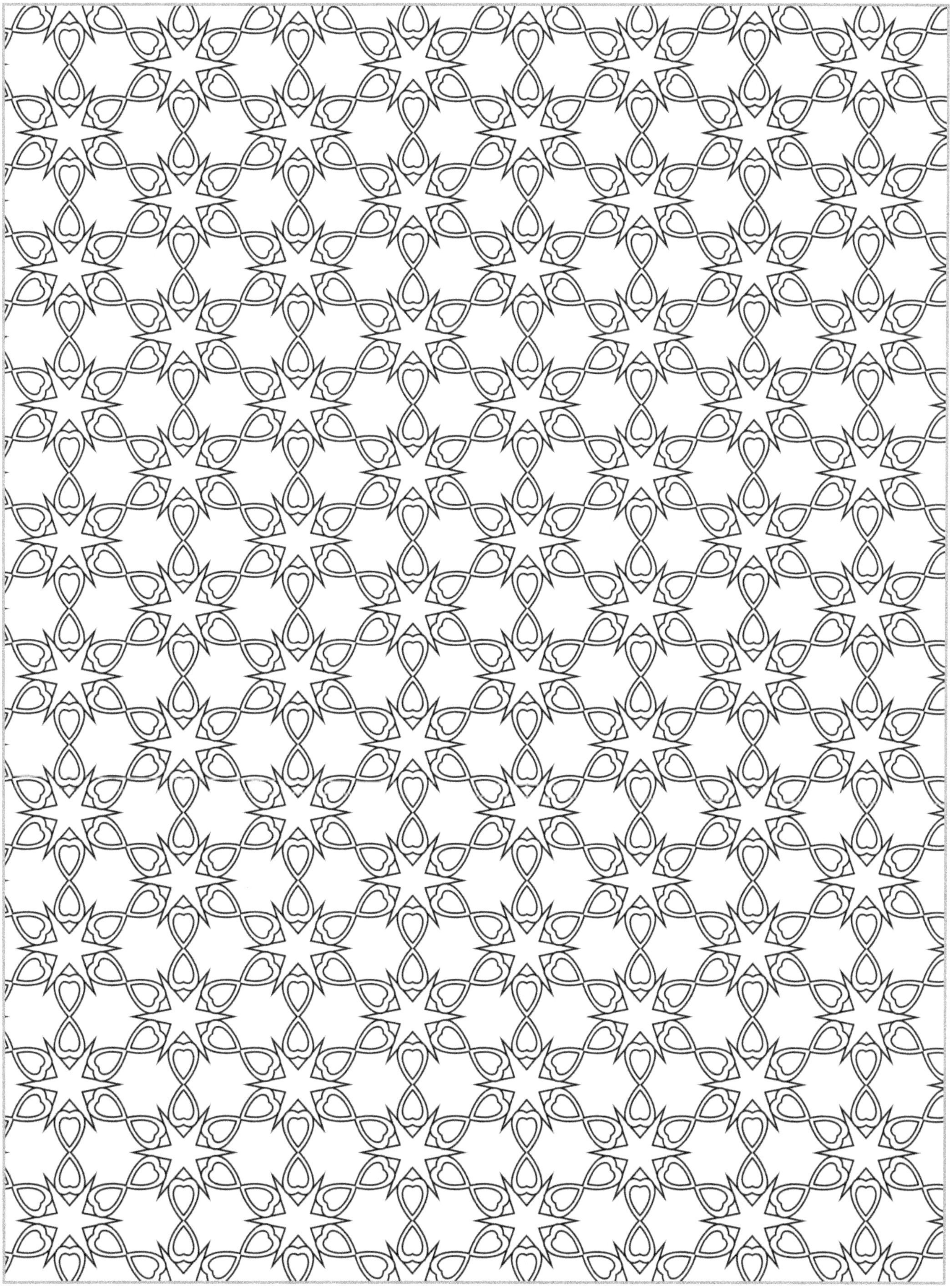

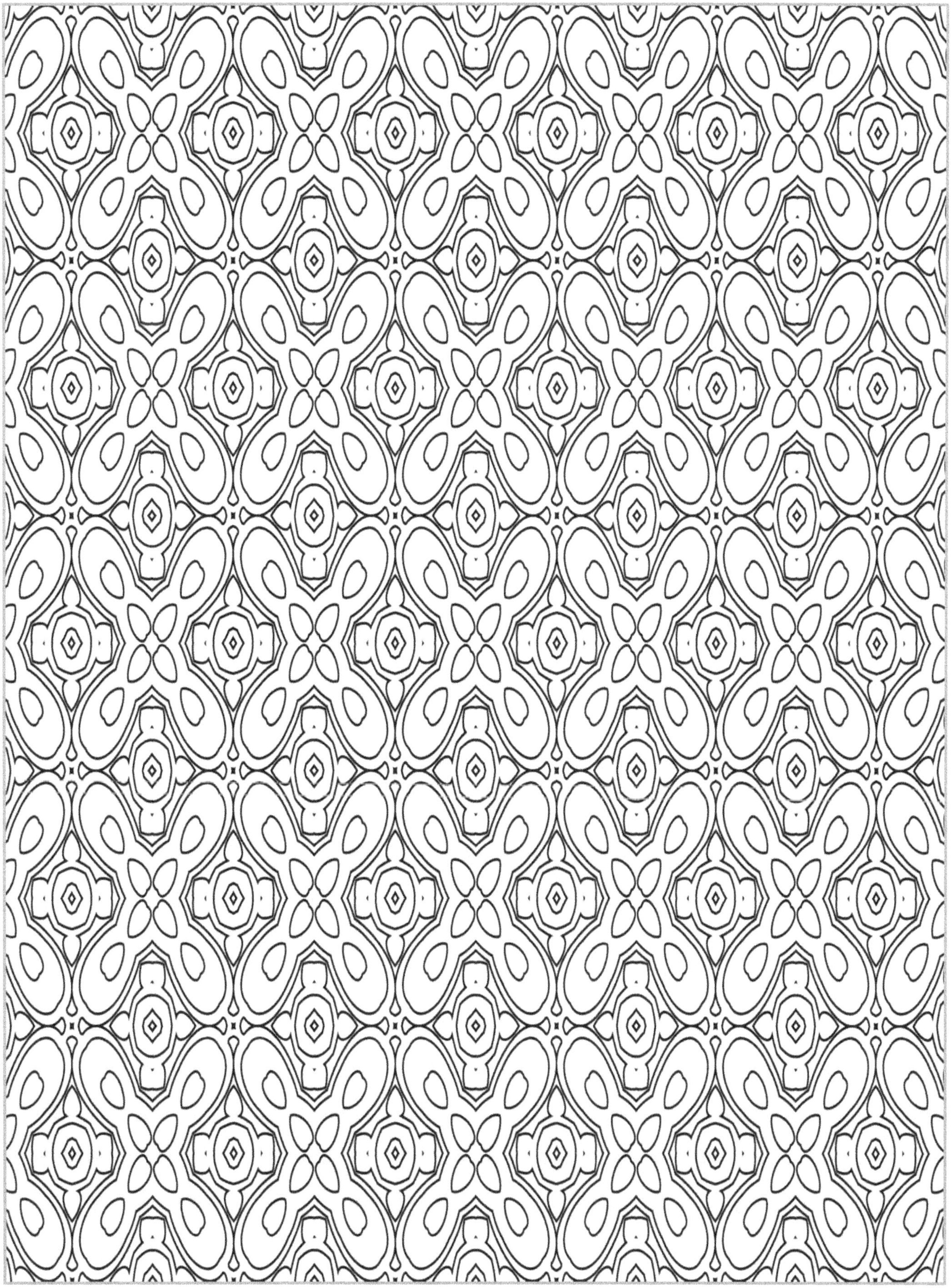

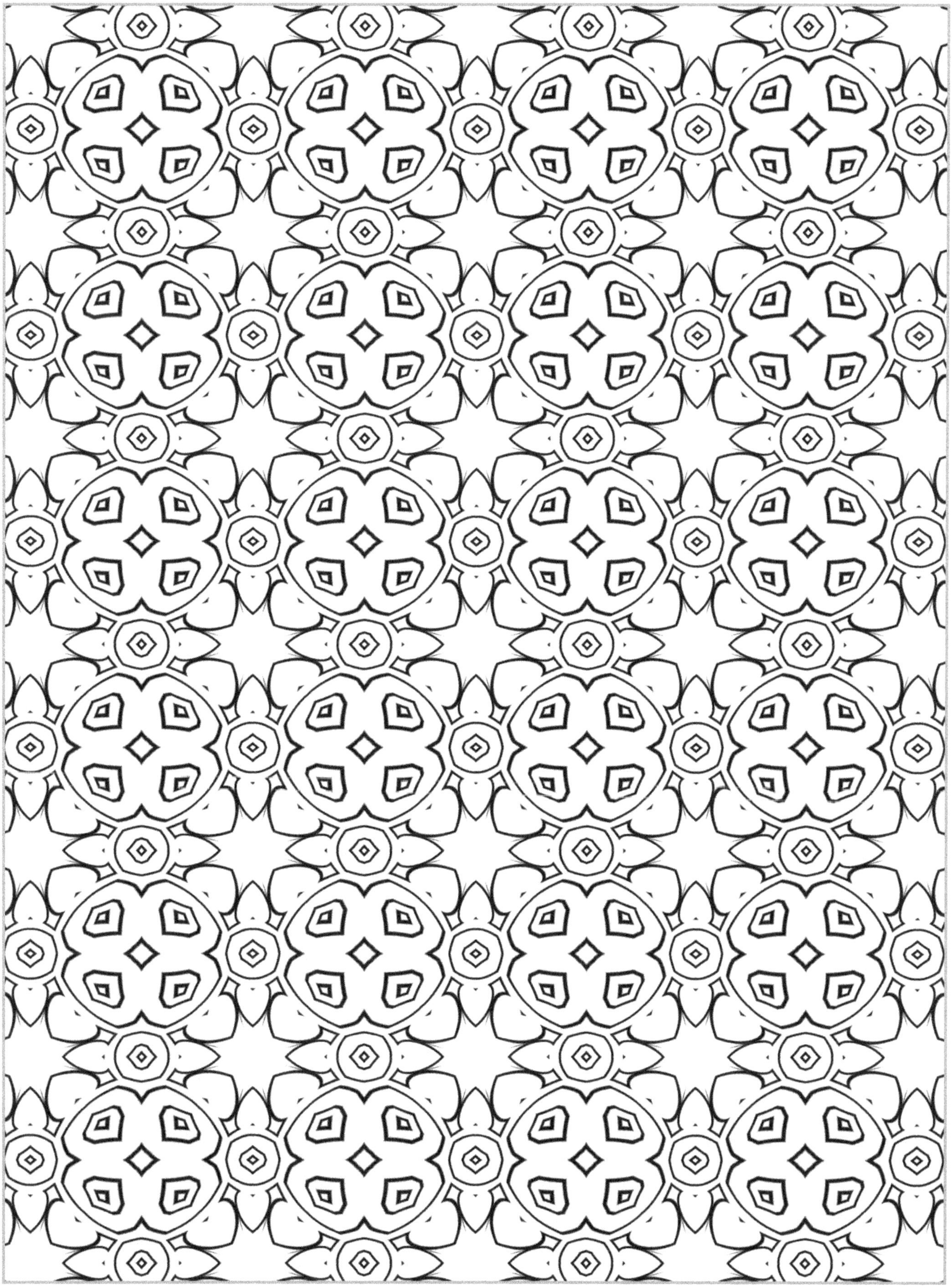

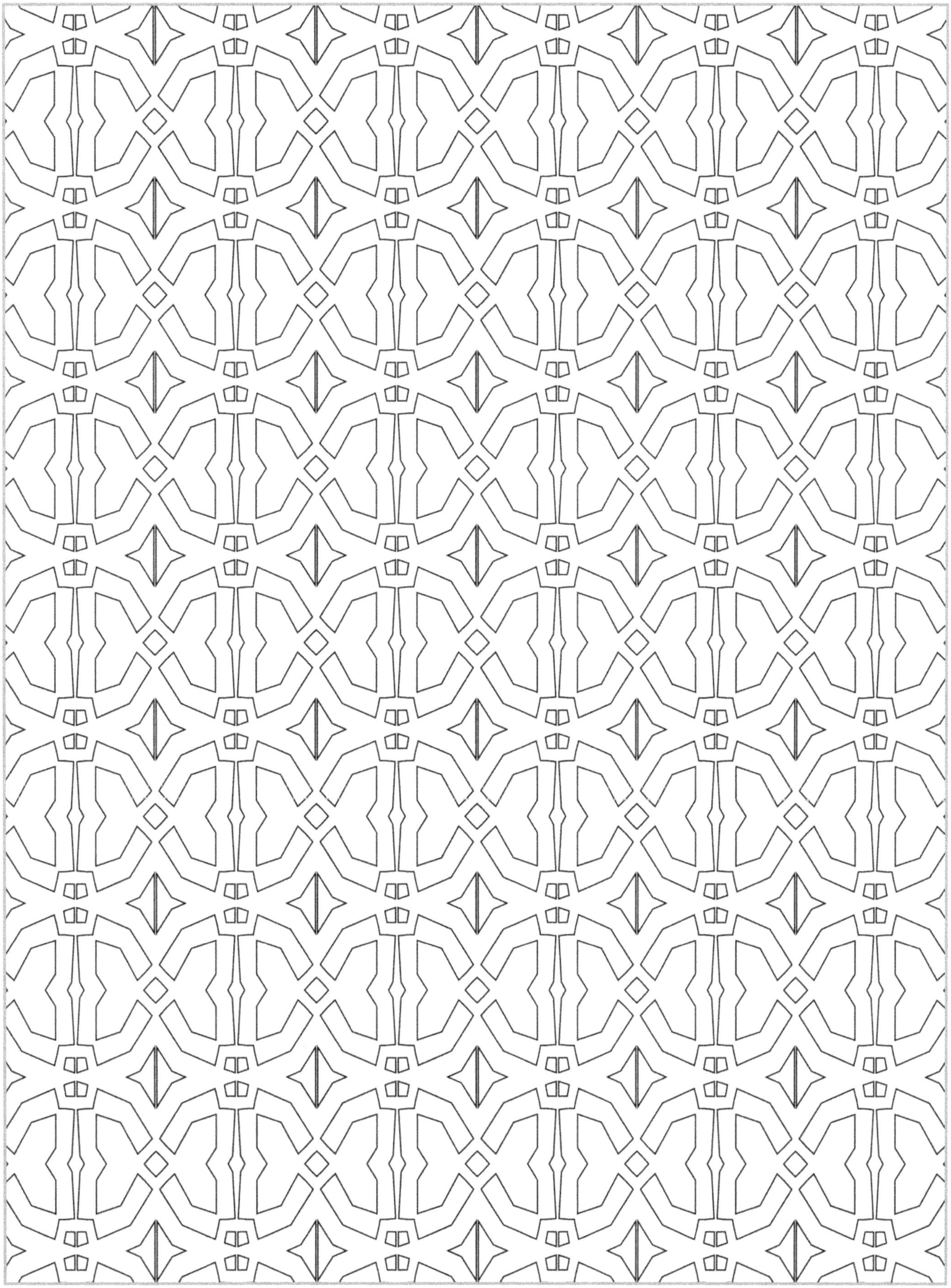

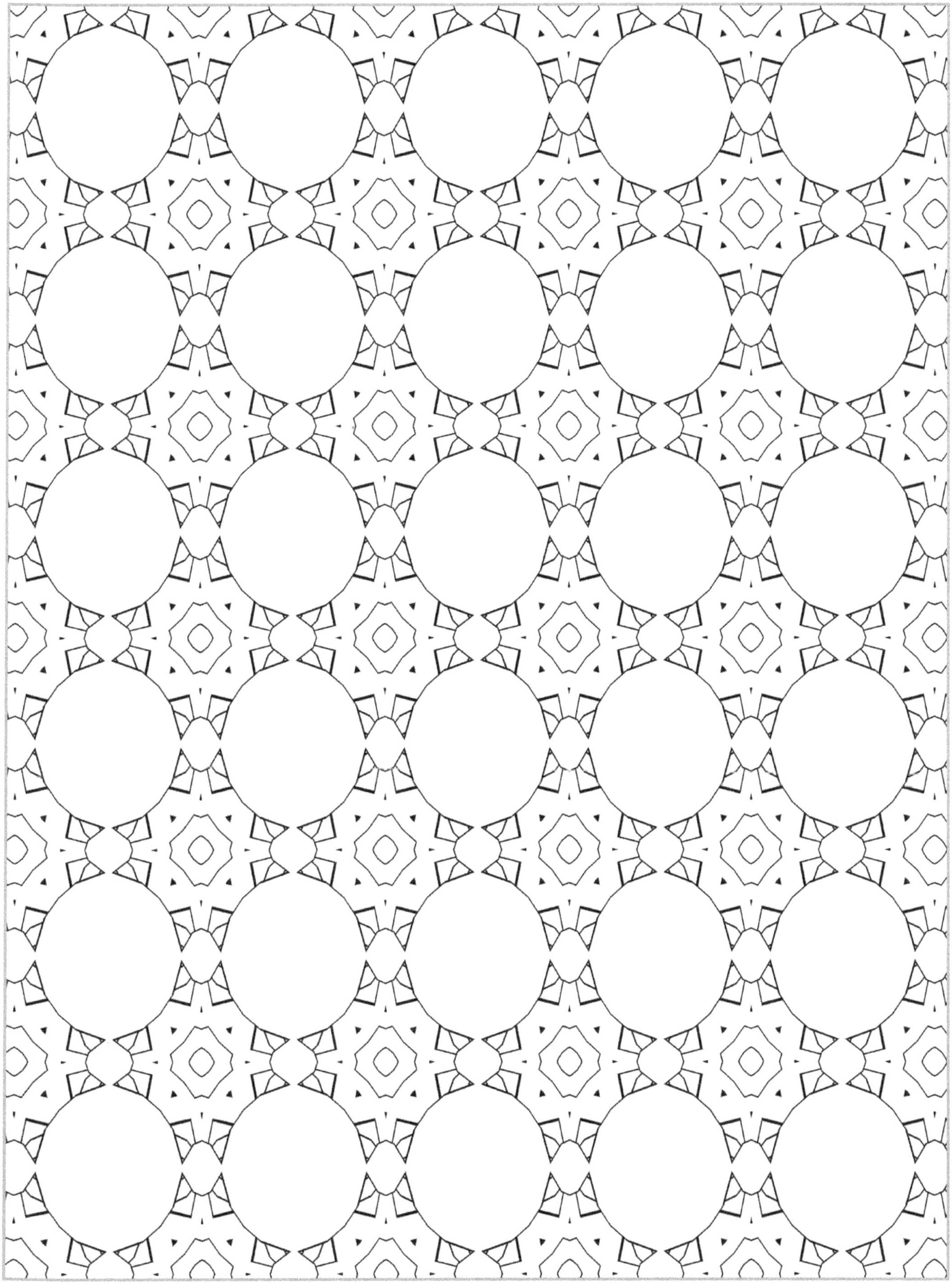

www.ingramcontent.com/pod-product-compliance
Lightning Source LLC
Chambersburg PA
CBHW080833180526
45168CB00006B/2662
* 9 7 8 1 5 1 5 0 2 4 5 3 8 *